The Lucent Library of Historical Eras

The 1960s
The Great Society:
The War on Poverty

Craig E. Blohm

LUCENT
BOOKS®

THOMSON
GALE

San Diego • Detroit • New York • San Francisco • Cleveland • New Haven, Conn. • Waterville, Maine • London • Munich

THOMSON
—★—
GALE

LIBRARY OF CONGRESS CATALOGING-IN-PUBLICATION DATA

Blohm, Craig E., 1948–
    The Great Society : America fights the war on poverty / by Craig E. Blohm.
        p. cm. — (The Lucent library of historical eras. 1960's)
Includes bibliographical references and index.
    ISBN 1-59018-385-1
    1. Poverty—Government policy—United States—History—20th century.
2. United States—Economic conditions—1961-1971. 3. United States—Social policy. I. Title. II. Series.
    HC110.P6B564 2004
    362.5'0973'09046—dc22
                                                            2004000457

Printed in the United States of America

Contents

Foreword

Looking back from the vantage point of the present, history can be viewed as a myriad of intertwining roads paved by human events. Some paths stand out—broad highways whose mileposts, even from a distance of centuries, are clear. The events that propelled the rise to power of Germany's Third Reich, its role in World War II, and its eventual demise, for example, are well defined and documented.

Other roads are less distinct, their route sometimes hidden from view. Modern legislatures may have developed from old tribal councils, for example, but the links between them are indistinct in places, open to discussion and interpretation.

The architecture of civilization—law, religion, art, science, and government—as well as the more everyday aspects of our culture—what we eat, what we wear—all developed along the historical roads and byways. In that progression can be traced every facet of modern life.

A broad look back along these roads reveals that many paths—though of vastly different character—seem to converge at a few critical junctions. These intersections are those great historical eras that echo over the long, steady course of human history, extending beyond the past and into the present.

These epic periods of time are the focus of Lucent's Library of Historical Eras. They shine through the mists of history like beacons, illuminated by a burst of creativity that propels events forward—so bright that we, from thousands of years away, can clearly see the chain of events leading to the present.

Each Lucent Library of Historical Eras consists of a set of books that highlight various aspects of these major eras. For example, the Elizabethan England library features volumes on Queen Elizabeth I and her court, Elizabethan theater, the great playwrights, and everyday life in Elizabethan London.

The mini-library approach allows for the division of each era into its most significant and most interesting parts and the exploration of those parts in depth. Also, social and cultural trends as well as illustrative documents and eyewitness accounts can be prominently featured in individual volumes.

Lucent's Library of Historical Eras presents a wealth of information to young readers. The lively narrative, fully documented primary and secondary source quotations, maps, photographs, sidebars, and annotated bibliographies serve as launching points for class discussion and further research.

In studying the great historical eras, students also develop a better understanding of our own times. What we learn from the past and how we apply it in the present may shape the future and may determine whether our era will be a guiding light to those traveling future roads.

Introduction:
Lyndon Johnson's Great Society

Lyndon Baines Johnson became president of the United States by way of an assassin's bullet in Dallas, Texas, on November 22, 1963. When John F. Kennedy was struck down that day, the New Frontier, Kennedy's vision for America, also died. Inheriting the highest office in the nation from a young, vigorous, and popular president, Johnson needed to establish his own vision for America. While Johnson vowed to continue the work of his predecessor, he also laid out the blueprint for what he hoped would be a legacy of social advances and domestic improvement. He called this proposal the Great Society.

Johnson's vision was nothing less than a sweeping plan to revitalize America. He envisioned a Great Society that would clean up America's air and water, beautify its highways, rebuild decaying inner cities, bring health care and educational opportunities to people of all ages, and address the problem of racial discrimination. But most of all, he wanted to launch a War on Poverty, which would become the cornerstone of the Great Society. Johnson grew up in a poor rural area of Texas, so he knew how poverty affected peoples' lives and spirits. As a teacher in the small, poverty-stricken town of Cotulla, Texas, in 1928, Johnson was moved by the poor children who showed up for his class. Often arriving at school hungry, these children had little to look forward to but a life of backbreaking work in the fields. "I was determined to help those poor little kids," Johnson later recalled. "I was determined to spark something inside them, to fill their souls with ambition and interest and belief in the future. I was determined to give them what they needed to make it in this world, to help them finish their education."[1] Thirty-five years later, what Johnson had wanted to do for the children of Cotulla, Texas, he hoped his War on Poverty could accomplish for every poor person in America.

Johnson also received inspiration from the New Deal, President Franklin D. Roosevelt's massive government program to fight poverty and joblessness during the Great Depression, the worst economic disaster of the twentieth century. The New

Deal created scores of new government agencies and projects designed to put the unemployed to work, help the poverty-stricken, and get the U.S. economy back on track. Johnson, a self-described New Dealer and an experienced wheeler-dealer in Congress, felt confident he could take Roosevelt's reforms even further.

But Johnson could not foresee a future in which the United States would become embroiled in a war half a world away, a war that would drain the money needed to fight poverty. Nor did he realize that the sheer enormity of the problem of poverty virtually guaranteed that his War on Poverty would not reach the lofty goals he set for it. At the outset, however, Johnson was optimistic: "I believe that thirty years from now Americans will look back upon these 1960s as the time of the great American Breakthrough—toward the victory of peace over war; toward the victory of prosperity over poverty; toward the victory of human rights over human wrongs; toward the victory of enlightened minds over darkness."[2] The Great Society, and especially the War on Poverty, were designed to secure these victories. But in war, expected victories do not always materialize, a lesson that Lyndon Johnson would ultimately learn the hard way.

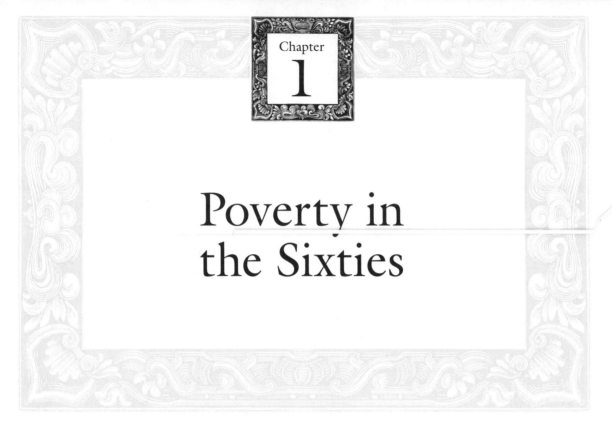

Poverty in the Sixties

At the beginning of the 1960s, America was, for most of its citizens, a land full of promise and prosperity. This economic abundance had begun fifteen years earlier, with a solemn ceremony held on the deck of the battleship USS *Missouri*. On September 1, 1945, delegates representing the empire of Japan signed official surrender documents aboard the historic warship, putting an end to the six-year global conflict known as World War II. With the twentieth century's most destructive war now over, America's fighting men would be returning home, eager to start families and get on with their lives.

Throughout the 1950s the U.S. economy boomed. A predicted postwar recession failed to materialize, and jobs were abundant. Americans began to spend money on the consumer goods that they had been forced to do without during the war. Shiny new cars sped down the lanes of a new interstate highway system that would soon span the nation. Suburban housing tracts seemed to spring up overnight as veterans took advantage of low interest government loans under legislation known as the GI Bill. In 1940, 40 percent of Americans owned their own homes; by 1960 that number had increased to 60 percent. Modern appliances such as refrigerators, stoves, and garbage disposals graced the kitchens of these new, if somewhat small, houses. And soon the roofs of those homes began sprouting antennae for the newest consumer gadget, television. At first dismissed as a passing fad, TV became so popular that by 1960 some 90 percent of all U.S. homes had a set. Although the screens were small and the pictures black-and-white, Americans loved television, because it reflected

their lives back to them through news, comedies, and dramas.

But there was something missing from the moving pictures that came into America's living rooms night after night. One segment

The Culture of Poverty

In his influential book, The Other America, *Michael Harrington wrote that the poor were becoming increasingly invisible to American society. Here, in an excerpt from that book, is one of Harrington's explanations for this invisibility.*

There are sociological and political reasons why poverty is not seen; and there are misconceptions and prejudices that literally blind the eye. . . . Here is the most familiar version of social blindness: "The poor are that way because they are afraid of work. And anyway they all have big cars. If they were like me (or my father or my grandfather), they could pay their own way. But they prefer to live on the dole and cheat the taxpayers."

This theory, usually thought of as a virtuous and moral statement, is one of the means of making it impossible for the poor ever to pay their way. There are, one must assume, citizens of the other America who choose impoverishment out of fear of work. . . . But the real explanation of why the poor are where they are is that they made the mistake of being born to the wrong parents, in the wrong section of the country, in the wrong industry, or in the wrong racial or ethnic group. Once that mistake has been made, they could have been paragons of will and morality, but most of them would never even have had a chance to get out of the other America.

There are two important ways of saying this: The poor are caught in a vicious circle; or, the poor live in a culture of poverty.

Author Michael Harrington believed that by the early 1960s America's poor had become a virtually invisible segment of society.

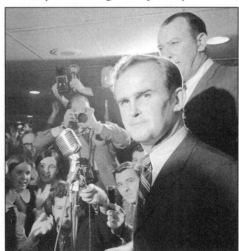

of society was rarely shown on television, just as it was seldom talked about, or even thought about, by the average American in the prosperous postwar years. That segment was the poor, and it was even given a name: The Other America.

The Literature of Poverty

In 1962 Michael Harrington, a socialist and a political activist, wrote a book entitled *The Other America: Poverty in the United States,* a groundbreaking study of poverty in America. The theme of the book is that in the United States there existed two Americas. One was the prosperous society that had arisen out of the post–World War II economic boom, where people became preoccupied with amassing consumer goods. "In all this," Harrington wrote, "there was an implicit assumption that the basic grinding economic problems had been solved in the United States. In this theory the nation's problems were no longer a matter of basic human needs, of food, shelter and clothing."[3] But Harrington discovered that

> there existed another America. In it dwelt somewhere between 40,000,000 and 50,000,000 citizens of this land. They were poor. They still are.
>
> To be sure, the other America is not impoverished in the same sense as those poor nations where millions cling to hunger as a defense against starvation. This country has escaped such extremes. That does not change the fact that tens of millions of

Americans are, at this very moment, maimed in body and spirit, existing at levels beneath those necessary for human decency. If these people are not starving, they are hungry, and sometimes fat with hunger, for that is what cheap foods do. They are without adequate housing and education and medical care.[4]

Harrington also observed that few middle-class Americans even noticed this impoverished segment of society. "The millions who are poor in the United States," wrote Harrington, "tend to become increasingly invisible. Here is a great mass of people, yet it takes an effort of the intellect and will even to see them."[5] *The Other America* received widespread public attention, bringing the plight of the poor to millions of Americans. But it was not the first book on poverty in modern America.

In 1958, four years before Harrington's book was published, the economist John Kenneth Galbraith wrote *The Affluent Society.* In this book, Galbraith declares that poverty survives even in an affluent society such as postwar America. He defines two categories of poverty: case poverty and insular poverty. Case poverty, according to Galbraith, can be found within every community, even prosperous ones. "Case poverty is the poor farm family with the junk-filled yard and the dirty children playing in the bare dirt. Or it is the gray-black hovel beside the railroad tracks. Or it is the basement dwelling in the alley."[6] People suffering from case poverty are poor due to a mental or physical disability that prevents them from keeping up with the economic advances of surrounding society.

The other type of poverty—insular poverty—Galbraith defines as poverty that exists in a geographic area or "island" wherein nearly everyone is poor. It is difficult to pinpoint a single cause of insular poverty. Race, poor education, lack of jobs, and the breakdown of family life all play a part. In the past, the blame for its existence was often placed on a poor physical environment, such as barren soil or few natural resources. Yet, Galbraith points out, some nondescript and resource-poor areas do prosper, while some beautiful and resource-rich areas do not.

One area of the United States that is rich in both beauty and natural resources hid some of the most grinding poverty to be found in the 1960s: Appalachia.

The Poor of Appalachia

Centered around the Appalachian Mountains in the eastern United States lies the region known as Appalachia. It is a broad geographical area spanning thirteen states from New York to Mississippi that was settled in the colonial era by European immigrants. In southern Appalachia the Blue Ridge and Great Smoky mountain chains, vast hardwood forests, and an abundance of colorful wildflowers give the region a haunting natural beauty. But hidden behind that beauty is an example of, in Michael Harrington's words, "The Other America." Coal mining had once been the lifeblood of the region, but automation took away jobs and left behind poverty and despair.

Economist John Kenneth Galbraith wrote The Affluent Society *in 1958 to explore the nature of poverty in postwar America.*

In the early 1960s some fifteen million people in Appalachia were poor. The region had higher infant mortality rates than the general population, fewer doctors, and provided inadequate education in decaying schools. Young people lucky enough to get at least a basic education left the region to find work in more prosperous areas of the country. Harry Caudill, a native of Appalachia who served as a congressman from Kentucky, wrote in 1962,

The Poverty of Appalachia

Rebecca Caudill grew up in southern Appalachia in a time before the coal mines, unions, and company towns came to this beautiful region of America. She returned in the late 1950s with her husband, hoping to see the idyllic mountain country of her youth. But what they found was poverty and desolation in the Appalachia that she had once called home. The following excerpt is from her book, My Appalachia.

Along any mountain road we traveled, we found disquieting signs—weatherbeaten shacks with large numbers of poorly clothed, dirty children playing in littered dooryards; neglected, dilapidated schoolhouses; tiny square-steepled churches from whose pulpits preachers faced empty benches and a few old ladies and shouted sermons about a life of idyllic ease in a beautiful alabaster city in the sky—a hereafter life to compensate for the hardships and sorrows of the earthly vale of tears.

An Appalachian woman sits outside her hut made of corrugated iron sheets.

From our friends we heard stories of mountain men who had been totally disabled in mine accidents and who were finding their Workmen's Compensation allotments pitifully insufficient to feed and clothe their large families; families that, after two or three generations on relief, were living aimless, hopeless lives of perpetual degrading poverty. We heard stories of able-bodied but unskilled men who could find no jobs and who, in order that their families might have food from relief agencies, had picked up and gone away, where no one knew.

One may walk . . . for days and rarely find a young man or woman. . . . One by one they slip away. A year after high-school diplomas are distributed, it is hard to find more than 4 or 5 percent of the graduates in their home counties. In the autumn of 1960 one high-school principal assured me that not a single graduate of his school in 1958, 1959 or 1960 was living in the county.[7]

For those who remained in Appalachia, life was hard. Food was often scarce, and routine medical care almost nonexistent. Dr. Sam Jackson visited the one-room shack of a family that had six children, and found four of them were retarded. "Those kids are probably retarded from malnutrition," Jackson said. "That youngest child's going to die—the one called Tommy—either of pneumonia or the sores and infections he's getting crawling around on the floor."[8] At the time, Tommy was seven years old and could not walk. The doctor's next stop brought him to a shack where he found a four-year-old girl named Lisa. Lisa seemed shy and said nothing in response to the doctor's questions. Upon examining her, Jackson found that Lisa's hearing had been so severely damaged by untreated infections that she could not hear words well enough to learn how to say them.

An editor of a Tennessee newspaper learned the truth of Harrington's *Other America* firsthand. He found it surprisingly close to home.

Ten minutes from my home, but a world away, I met this family. . . . Cleanliness seems fruitless to them— perhaps they don't try, perhaps they don't know how or understand the need. They want a warmer place for the winter but the father was injured on his last job and who wants to rent to a nonproductive family? They're not bitter, or jealous, just hopeless. They ask for nothing—but they seem to be waiting for some sort of miracle to release them from the situation in which they are caught.[9]

Poverty in the sixties was not limited to the rural poor. It could also be found in the ghettos of such large cities as New York, Chicago, and Detroit.

Urban Poverty in the Sixties

The rural poor have always looked to the cities, especially the large industrial cities of the North, as gateways to employment and life in America's mainstream. During World War II, a shortage of workers in defense plants led to a great migration of poor African Americans from the South to the North. More than a million black workers left the South to build airplanes, tanks, and munitions in northern and western factories. But while blacks could find jobs, they had difficulty finding housing. Segregation kept blacks from renting housing in white neighborhoods. As more blacks moved north, the urban ghettos in which they were forced to live became more and more crowded. Public schools were also overcrowded, and black students often fared poorly because their parents, educated in inferior southern schools, could not help them.

By the early 1960s some 4 million African Americans had migrated north. Before long, however, employment—the reason that African Americans had moved north in the first place—began to decline. Many jobs were relocated from the cities to the suburbs; others were eliminated as automation in factories became more widespread. This left many urban blacks unemployed and stranded in deteriorating ghettos where drug use and crime began to rise. The outward appearance of a black ghetto in the sixties may have differed from city to city, but according to Michael Harrington, inside they were remarkably similar:

> In Los Angeles, the Negro slum sprawls like everything else. The only obvious thing about it is that the streets, like the streets of the poor everywhere, are badly paved. It takes a little while to learn that the innocent, individual houses are often as rotten inside as any tenement. In Chicago, on the South Side, there is the unmistakable feeling of the great metropolitan ghetto: high buildings, honky tonks, and on the fringes, a sense of tension in one of the most explosive racial situations in the country. . . . To live in Harlem (in New York City) is to be a Negro; to be a Negro is to participate in a culture of poverty and fear that goes far deeper than any law for or against discrimination. [10]

In New York City in the 1950s, black unemployment was double of that for whites, and black employees routinely received lower pay than their white counterparts. In 1961 the infant mortality rate in Harlem was 45.2 per thousand, compared with 25.7 per thousand for all of New York City. Nearly a quarter of a million people lived in Harlem's 3.5-square-mile area. Most of the housing was crowded and in poor condition, with some 44 percent of the dwellings in need of significant repair. And yet rents were high, set by slum landlords ("slumlords") who knew that the poor blacks of New York had few housing alternatives from which to choose.

Like all inner-city ghettos, Harlem was a nucleus of urban poverty, a "dark ghetto" according to Kenneth B. Clark, a consultant for Harlem Youth Opportunities Unlimited in the early 1960s. "The symptoms of lower-class society afflict the dark ghettos of America—low aspiration, poor education, family instability, illegitimacy, unemployment, crime, drug addiction, and alcoholism, frequent illness and early death." [11] The significant role of drugs in the ghetto was described to Clark by a twenty-six-year-old addict who expresses despair over his own situation, but hope for future generations:

> I was just born black, poor and uneducated. . . . I'm poor and all I can look forward to is what I can get out of this bag [of drugs]. That's the only thrill in life for me, you know. I've never had anything, no opportunity, you know,

to get any money, no nothing. All I can look forward to is what I can get out of this bag, and that's nothing really. . . . I think I can enjoy working, and raising a family, like the next man, but this is all they left me. I can't work, so I must steal. . . . I don't think anything can be done to correct it. Me, because I'm too far gone on it, you know. But, I mean, for my brothers and sisters, you know, people that are coming up younger than I, you know, they can do something. Give them a better education and better job opportunities. [12]

Black children who lived in urban ghettos faced many problems, including drugs and violent crime.

Education and job opportunities were the dual foundations upon which the poverty programs of the sixties would be built. But first the government had to determine the extent of poverty in the United States.

Measuring Poverty

By the early 1960s social scientists and economists were beginning to realize that poverty in America was a larger problem than previously thought. What surprised them was how much they did not know about poverty. Many questions arose: Who are the poor? How many poor Americans are there? And how do we determine who is poor and who is not?

The basic measure of poverty, called poverty thresholds, was developed in 1963 by Mollie Orshansky, a research analyst in the Social Security Administration. These thresholds were based on the annual income a family needed in 1963 to purchase an adequate supply of food. Orshansky knew that a typical family of three or more spent about one-third of its income on groceries. Taking into consideration other necessary expenses, she decided that multiplying this amount by three would result in an income level at which a family could live a satisfactory, if not lavish, life. If a family fell below this level they could be considered poor. Using her formula Orshansky developed a chart of 124 poverty thresholds, taking into account family size, ages of family members, the number of children, and other factors. Orshansky's thresholds were not meant to measure how much money one needed to live well. She commented that,

Measuring Poverty

Weighted average nonfarm poverty thresholds at the economy level and at the low cost level for calendar year 1963.

Size of family unit	Thresholds at economy level in 1963*	Thresholds at low-cost level in 1969**	Ratio
1	$1,539	—	—
Under age 65	$1,580	$1,885	1.19
Aged 65 or older	$1,470	$1,745	1.19
2	$1,988	—	—
Head under age 65	$2,050	$2,715	1.32
Head aged 65 or older	$1,850	$2,460	1.33
3	$2,440	$3,160	1.30
4	$3,130	$4,005	1.28
5	$3,685	$4,675	1.27
6	$4,135	$5,250	1.27
7 or more	$5,090	$6,395	1.26

* Poverty thresholds under the 1963 definition.   ** Known until 1969 as the near-poverty or low-income thresholds.

while it was "not possible to state unequivocally 'how much is enough,' it should be possible to assert with confidence, how much, on an average, is too little." [13]

Orshansky's findings were first published in January 1965. In that year the annual income level below which a family was considered poor was $3,223. This may seem like a small amount of money for a family to live on, especially compared to the 2003 level of $18,400. But many families had much less. In Detroit, poor families receiving government assistance had to make do with an annual income of $1,920. For these families, fresh fruits and vegetables were a rare luxury; new clothing, even such necessary apparel as raincoats and boots, was out of the question. Living conditions were often substandard, with one out of four families occupying housing that had no running water, and even more lacking enough beds for all family members.

As the prosperous decade of the 1950s turned into the new and optimistic decade of the 1960s, most Americans were still unaware of the crisis of poverty that affected some 39 million of their fellow citizens. But that was about to change with the election of a young, vigorous president who would set the stage for America's War on Poverty.

Origins of the War on Poverty

Michael Harrington's *The Other America* had a significant effect on the way Americans were beginning to think about poverty. One man who was influenced by the ideas presented in the book was the president of the United States, John F. Kennedy, who had entered office the previous year. Kennedy asked economist Walter Heller to create an antipoverty program for the 1964 legislative session. Growing international tensions of the Cold War kept the president from pursuing his antipoverty agenda, and little progress was made. When Kennedy was tragically assassinated on November 22, 1963, the task of fighting poverty fell to his successor, Lyndon B. Johnson.

In Kennedy's unfulfilled poverty program Johnson saw the seeds of an idea that he could expand into a major component of his own domestic social agenda. Johnson's grand design for reshaping America included not only fighting poverty, but the creation of other programs that would beautify the nation, provide help for senior citizens, create jobs for the masses, furnish housing for the homeless, and generally create a better America. To come up with a memorable name for this far-reaching plan, Johnson's speechwriter, Richard Goodwin, consulted historian Eric F. Goldman. Goldman later recalled his suggestion "that in terms of a popular slogan, the goal of 'post-affluent' America was probably best caught by the title of . . . [a]

book of some years back, *The Good Society.*"[14] It was Goodwin's idea to change the phrase to "the Great Society." Actually, Johnson did not particularly care for the name at first. But "the Great Society" stuck and became the catchphrase for Johnson's administration.

On May 22, 1964, Johnson first used the name Great Society publicly during his commencement address to the graduating class at the University of Michigan at Ann Arbor. In his address he presented his audience with a utopian vision of the kind of America that would be created by the Great Society:

The Great Society rests on abundance and liberty for all. It demands an end to poverty and racial injustice, to which we are totally committed in our time. But that is just the beginning. The Great Society is a place where every child can find knowledge to enrich his mind and to enlarge his talents. It is a place where leisure is a welcome chance to build and reflect, not a feared cause of boredom and restlessness. It is a place where the city of man serves not only the needs of the body and the demands of commerce but the desire for beauty and the hunger for community. It is a place where man can renew contact with nature. It is a place which honors creation for its own sake and for what it adds to the understanding of the race. It is a place where men are more concerned with the quality of

their goals than with the quantity of their goods. . . . Will you join in the battle to build the Great Society?[15]

Johnson's speech was enthusiastically received by the crowd of more than eighty thousand people. On the flight back to Washington, Johnson was exhilarated by the feeling that he had the support of the nation for his Great Society. But while his optimistic vision was cheered at Ann Arbor, it was not shared by the majority of the population. A poll showed that 85 percent of Americans felt that poverty would never be completely abolished, while only 9 percent said that such an outcome was possible. Johnson's War on Poverty would be an uphill battle.

Johnson's Program

Walter Heller met with the new president shortly after Johnson took office, and described Kennedy's poverty program to him. Johnson's reaction was enthusiastic: "That's my kind of program. We should push ahead full-tilt on this project."[16] Johnson was truly interested in fighting poverty in America. But he was also mindful of the coming election in November 1964. "I've got to be thinking about my future. . . . to put my stamp on this Administration in order to run for office."[17] But what form would that stamp take? At the time no one in the Johnson administration had any concrete plans for fighting poverty.

Around the Christmas holiday in 1963 Johnson invited a group of advisers to his

Presenting War on Poverty

On March 16, 1964, President Johnson introduced the War on Poverty in a special message to Congress. The following excerpts from this message are from the Fordham University website.

Because it is right, because it is wise, and because, for the first time in our history, it is possible to conquer poverty, I submit, for the consideration of the Congress and the country, the Economic Opportunity Act of 1964. The Act does not merely expand old programs or improve what is already being done. It charts a new course. It strikes at the causes, not just the consequences of poverty. It can be a milestone in our one-hundred-eighty year search for a better life for our people. . . .

We are fully aware that this program will not eliminate all the poverty in America in a few months or a few years. Poverty is deeply rooted and its causes are many. But this program will show the way to new opportunities for millions of our fellow citizens. It will provide a lever with which we can begin to open the door to our prosperity for those who have been kept outside. It will give us the chance to test our weapons, to try our energy and ideas and imagination for the many battles yet to come. As conditions change, and as experience illuminates our difficulties, we will be prepared to modify our strategy. And this program is much more than a beginning. Rather it is a commitment. It is a total commitment by this President, and this Congress, and this nation, to pursue victory over the most ancient of mankind's enemies.

ranch in Texas, where they discussed how best to approach the daunting task of creating a program to fight poverty. The group included Walter Heller, budget director Kermit Gordon, and special assistants to the president, Bill Moyers and Jack Valenti. The group first suggested that the poverty program begin on a small scale, with a series of demonstration projects in a limited number of cities. But Johnson had bigger plans. "I was certain," he recalled, "that we could not start small and hope to propel a program through Congress. It had to be big and bold and hit the whole nation with real impact."[18] The group at the Texas ranch foresaw the need for a budget of around $1 billion to fight poverty, both directly through community programs and indirectly through government agencies whose work contributed in some way to helping the poor.

It was at these holiday meetings that a title for Johnson's poverty program was

In 1964 President Lyndon Johnson launched his War on Poverty, a program designed to eradicate the problem.

industry, and on campuses to lend their talents to a massive effort to eliminate the evil."[19] Johnson announced the establishment of the War on Poverty in his first State of the Union address on January 8, 1964. Before a joint session of Congress, he proclaimed:

> This administration today, here and now, declares unconditional war on poverty in America. . . . Poverty is a national problem, requiring improved national organization and support. But this attack, to be effective, must also be organized at the State and local level and must be supported and directed by State and local efforts. . . . Our joint Federal–local effort must pursue poverty, pursue it wherever it exists—in city slums and small towns, in sharecropper shacks or in migrant worker camps, on Indian Reservations, among whites as well as Negroes, among the young as well as the aged, in the boom towns and in the depressed areas. . . . Our aim is not only to relieve the symptom of poverty, but to cure it and, above all, to prevent it.[20]

decided upon. Several names were considered, but none carried the weight or importance Johnson felt his program deserved. After much discussion the name War on Poverty was officially adopted. "It had its disadvantages," Johnson later remembered. "The military image carried with it connotations of victories and defeats that could prove misleading. But I wanted to rally the nation, to sound a call to arms which would stir people in the government, in private

The War on Poverty was now officially established, but it needed someone to lead the battles that lay ahead. Johnson chose R. Sargent Shriver, John F. Kennedy's brother-in-law and director of the Peace Corps, a volunteer organization that assists people in underdeveloped countries to improve their living conditions. The Peace Corps had been the most successful and highly respected agency of Kennedy's administration. Shriver had the qualities Johnson was looking for: organizational skills, experience in dealing with Congress, and, perhaps most important, the respect of the senators and congressmen with whom he dealt. But it would take all of Johnson's powers of persuasion and pressure tactics to convince Shriver to join his team.

On the last day of January 1964 Johnson told Shriver, "we're getting this war against poverty started. I'd like you to think about that, because I'd like you to run that program for us."[21] Shriver, knowing how much work he still had to do in the Peace Corps, did not immediately answer. At 10:00 A.M. the next day, February 1, Shriver's telephone rang. "What do you think about that war against poverty?" the president asked. Shriver had to admit that he had not given it any

thought. "Sarge," Johnson continued, "I'd like to have a press conference today at noon, and I'd like to announce you as the head of my new program."[22] Shriver asked for a week to think it over and hung up, but Johnson was persistent; he called again at 11:30. "You just have to understand, Sargent, that this is your President speaking, and I'm going to announce you as the head of the war against poverty." At that, Shriver told his wife, "Looks as if I'm going to be the new head of the war against poverty."[23]

Beginning the War

As Shriver started his new position, he soon realized that "nobody really knew how to fight poverty."[24] So his first job was to assemble a task force to determine just how to wage the War on Poverty. In typical fashion, Shriver wasted no time, calling the

President Johnson (in chair) nominated Peace Corps director R. Sargent Shriver (left) to lead America's war against poverty.

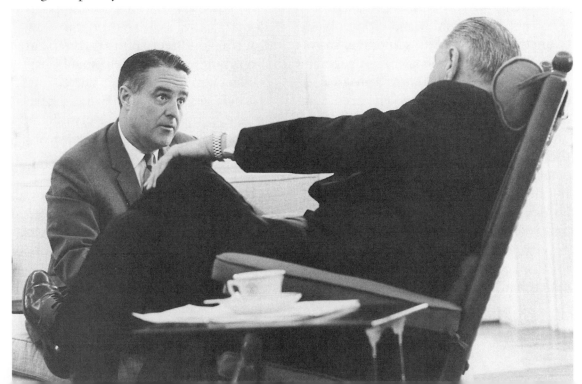

initial meeting of his task force on February 2, the day after he was appointed. Although this first session was small, over the next month and a half more than 130 people attended various task force meetings to give Shriver advice and information. Businessmen, state and federal government officials, teachers, social workers, and others provided input to the task force. Among those that Shriver invited was Michael Harrington, author of *The Other America*.

Johnson had given Shriver the job of creating a bill that would introduce the major programs of the War on Poverty, and then shepherding the bill through Congress. Once Shriver had received this mandate, Johnson stepped back and let his poverty director work out the details. Frank Mankiewicz, a Peace Corps official who had discussed poverty with Shriver, recalls a meeting with Johnson: "We went over and outlined some of the things we had. And as I recall, he listened rather impassively and didn't object to anything."[25] Johnson sometimes made a few suggestions of his own, but generally he followed the committee's progress as it worked out its program. The president did make it clear, however, that the program should aid the poor by improving their education, job skills, and access to employment, not by simply giving money. In other words, the War on Poverty would provide "a hand up, not a handout," a phrase that would become associated with Johnson's poverty programs.

Community action programs, or CAPs, which had been discussed by the Texas ranch group during the Christmas holiday meetings, were on the agenda for inclusion in the bill. The CAPs would assess the needs of the poor in a neighborhood and create local programs to address those needs. They would administer funding and work closely with people in the local community. Initially, Shriver was skeptical that such a program could be effective soon enough to provide the practical results that Congress would expect. He candidly told a colleague, "It'll never fly."[26] Changes would have to be made in order to be sure the CAPs would pass congressional review. Johnson recalled the progress the task force was making:

Soon other ideas began to take their place beside community action in the emerging legislative proposal: programs to give a special educational head start to children of deprived backgrounds; plans to train school dropouts for productive jobs; a blueprint to draw on the volunteer spirit of American youth; new ways to help small businessmen in the slums get started and to help impoverished farmers keep going; programs to enable students from low-income families to work while they pursued an education.[27]

Not every idea proposed was approved, and there were the inevitable arguments and disagreements within the task force as each member sought to champion his own pet proposals. But just six weeks after the task force first met, the poverty bill was ready. It

President Johnson holds a copy of the Economic Opportunity Act after signing it into law in August 1964. The act served as a blueprint for the War on Poverty.

was called the Economic Opportunity Act of 1964, and Johnson immediately approved it and sent it to Congress on March 16, 1964. Hearings on the bill began the next day and continued for four months. During this time members of the Johnson administration traveled the country making speeches in support of the War on Poverty. Johnson and his wife Lady Bird toured the Midwest and Appalachia to personally visit with the poor people who would benefit from the poverty programs. Media interest soared and stories about the poor appeared in newspapers and magazines.

On July 23, 1964, the Economic Opportunity Act passed the Senate by a vote of 61 to 34. Two weeks later the House passed the bill 226 to 185. Johnson signed the bill into law on August 24, 1964, at a ceremony in the White House Rose Garden. At the signing, Johnson said, "Today for the first time in all the history of the human race, a great nation is able to make and is willing to make a commitment to eradicate poverty among its people."[28]

The Economic Opportunity Act

The Economic Opportunity Act, officially known as Public Law 88-452, was the battle plan for the War on Poverty. The war would be fought on several fronts:

A Trip to Appalachia

As Congress debated the poverty bill, Johnson traveled the country in an effort to keep his plan for the poor in the headlines. In Appalachia, one of the most economically depressed regions of the nation, the president met a man named Tom Fletcher. To Johnson, Fletcher exemplified the plight of the poor all across America. Johnson recalls the visit in his memoir, The Vantage Point.

I will not forget the man whose home I visited on the banks of Rock Castle Creek on a mountainside in eastern Kentucky. His name was Tom Fletcher. His house was a tar-papered, three room shack which he shared with his wife and their eight children. I sat on the porch with him while he described the struggle he had to support them all on $400 a year. He regretted more than anything else that his two oldest children had already dropped out of school, and he was worried that the same fate would overtake the others. So was I. The tragic inevitability of the endless cycle of poverty was summed up in that man's fear: poverty forcing children out of school and destroying their best chance to escape the poverty of their fathers. . . .

My determination was reinforced that day to use the powers of the Presidency to the fullest extent I could, to persuade America to help all its Tom Fletchers. They lived in the hollows of Appalachia and the hill country of central Texas, in swamp and desert, in cane brake and forest, and in the crumbling slums of every American city and every state. They were black and they were white, of every religion and background and national origin. And they were 35 million strong.

President Johnson meets with a poor family during a 1964 visit to Appalachia.

jobs, education, community action, and incentives for businesses to hire the unemployed. The act called for the creation of antipoverty programs to be the frontline units conducting the war. A Job Corps would be formed to give the unemployed education and marketable skills. Community action programs would bring to reality the concept of local community organizations working to eliminate poverty in their neighborhoods. A domestic organization similar to Kennedy's Peace Corps would recruit volunteers to work with local residents in the poorest regions of America.

The Economic Opportunity Act described in detail how these antipoverty agencies should be organized, administered, and funded. In doing so it produced a fundamental change in the federal government's fiscal relations with American nonprofit organizations. Funds would go directly from the federal government to the organizations, bypassing state and local governments.

As might be expected, this was a controversial feature of the Economic Opportunity Act. Many governors thought that they should have control over what was going on in their state and be able to block activities that they felt were not in the state's best interests. But proponents of the act countered that the War on Poverty was a national endeavor and that governors should

not be allowed to interfere with its operation. In fact, the act included a provision to allow governors to veto the establishment of certain poverty programs within their state. However, in 1965 this was modified to allow a federal reversal of a governor's veto if it was determined that the poverty program in question was operating within the purposes of the act.

The Economic Opportunity Act also proposed the creation of an agency called the Office of Economic Opportunity (OEO) to coordinate the Johnson administration's antipoverty programs. Shriver would become the director of the Office of Economic Opportunity and would report directly to Johnson. This assured that the decision-making functions of the office remained under the watchful eye of the president rather than Congress, which could add unwelcome complications to the task of fighting poverty.

With its initial budget set at $962.5 million, the OEO heralded the beginning of the War on Poverty. When warned by Michael Harrington that the money would not be enough, Sargent Shriver replied, "I don't know about you, Mr. Harrington, but this will be my first experience at spending a billion dollars, and I'm quite excited about it." [29] Indeed, the excitement was building within the War on Poverty as the first programs began to take shape.

Chapter

3

Helping in the Community

The idea of people in a community organizing to help their neighbors is as old as the United States itself. In colonial times, for example, the church was the institution that looked after the welfare of those in the community who were less fortunate. Settlement houses, developed during the industrial boom of the eighteenth century, offered services to the community in an effort to improve the health, education, and living conditions of the residents in the local neighborhood. During the Great Depression of the 1930s, many federal assistance programs were administered by state and local governments.

The modern incarnation of community action as a way to help the poor help themselves originated with the Ford Foundation, an organization that grants funds to help find solutions to pressing social problems. In the early 1960s the foundation funded several pilot programs that sought to alleviate inner-city poverty through locally administered programs. The Kennedy administration had also used local community action to combat juvenile delinquency. These were revolutionary concepts for their time. "The idea [was] that government leaders should plan with the poor, not for the poor . . . that comprehensive community action should replace piecemeal approaches." [30]

Fighting Poverty Locally

From the beginning of the War on Poverty it was determined that people in the local communities should play a major role in fighting poverty in their own neighborhoods. In November 1963 David Hackett, a member of the Department of Justice who had worked on Kennedy's juvenile delinquency program, wrote a memo to Walter Heller suggesting a unique approach to creating a national poverty program. The memo said that President Johnson should establish five poverty projects for residents of inner-city slums, migrant workers, Native Americans, people who were institutionalized, and residents of other depressed areas. Locally based, these projects would become the underlying framework for a national poverty program.

The responsibility for developing the projects was given to the Bureau of the Budget. After reviewing the proposal the bureau made several recommendations: It

Community Action at Work

Total Action Against Poverty, known as TAP, is a community action organization that has been helping people in the Roanoke, Virginia, area for more than three decades. The following is an excerpt from Community Action at Work: TAP's Thirty-Year War on Poverty *by Elizabeth Brand.*

"TAP opened up a lot of hope for the people," states Martha Ogden, who in 1965 volunteered to work for TAP in organizing her northwest Roanoke neighborhood. "TAP taught people how to ask for things they wanted. . . . In my neighborhood, the kids were always playing in the street. They didn't have anywhere else to play. They'd play kickball and baseball. And somebody was always getting hurt. We needed a park, and we decided to go to the city and ask for money to buy land for a park. The place we wanted was a lot of dangerous, dilapidated, rat-infested housing, and real old people lived there. We had a hard time convincing the old people that there were better places for them to live, but we did.

"So we went to the city manager and told him what we wanted. He told us, 'We know you want a lot of things.' . . . and I told him, 'We've been paying out taxes all these many years, and it's time for you to put some of the tax money back out in the community.' He sat up straight and said, 'I heard what you said. I can't undo the past, but we can start. You just give me a list of the things that you feel are important.'

"Well, we had so many things that we needed. But I felt at that time that we really needed a park. They had built the Hurt [housing projects] nearby. There were a lot of kids and no place to play. We asked for a park and got it."

suggested that the number of programs be increased from five to ten and proposed the creation of what it called development corporations as the basis for local poverty operations. These corporations would have the responsibility of deciding which among various local poverty proposals would receive federal funding, and would then oversee the operation of the local programs once they were established. Initial funding of the program would be $500 million. One change the bureau made was the name of the program: No one really liked the sound of the name "development corporation." It eventually was replaced by the phrase Community Action Program (CAP), which became the official title of the community-based initiative on poverty. "The plan had the sound of something brand new and even faintly radical," recalled Johnson. "Actually it was based on one of the oldest ideas of our democracy, as old as the New England town meeting—self-determination at the local level." [31]

Budget Director Kermit Gordon was not sure his agency knew enough about poverty to wisely spend the half a billion dollars allotted for the Community Action Program. After several meetings with people knowledgeable about funding poverty programs, such as Paul Ylvisaker of the Ford Foundation, Gordon finally "had a clear notion of what we were trying to do." [32] He realized that poverty differed from one community to another and that local governments should work with private community groups to fight poverty.

The importance of input from the local community was embodied in the phrase "maximum feasible participation." This meant that the poor people themselves should have as much voice as possible in the poverty programs that would be established to help them. "Maximum feasible participation" was coined by Richard Boone, a member of the planning committee, who worked hard to get the phrase to be a part of the new program. During one meeting, Boone repeated it so often that a colleague remarked, "You have used that phrase four or five times now." Boone replied, "How many times do I have to use it before it becomes part of the program?" "Oh, a couple of times more," [33] came the joking answer. Eventually the concept of maximum feasible participation did make its way into the poverty bill. But it was not without controversy. As Sam Brown, a consultant to the Peace Corps recalls:

Citizen participation, the belief in the "maximum feasible participation" of poor people in the decision-making process came across as a very democratic idea when you read about it in the legislative language. But when citizen participation turned out to be a rent strike in Chicago over rats in public housing, a bail bond project in Tulsa, a campaign in West Virginia to make the coal companies pay compensation to black lung victims, and organizing welfare recipients in Philadelphia to get what was entitled

Sargent Shriver appears before a Congressional committee to gain support for the War on Poverty. Shriver believed that community action was essential to the success of the war.

to them by law, well, that was a different ball game. A great many people didn't like the score. [34]

Sargent Shriver's experience with the Peace Corps helped confirm his belief that community action should be an important part of the War on Poverty:

There were many, many things in the Peace Corps which were applicable to the War on Poverty . . . [especially] the approach which we in the Peace Corps called "community development." In fact, doing community development

in Ecuador is, philosophically and substantially, no different than doing the same thing in some West Virginia hollow. . . . The concept of going into Ecuador to try to help people decide their own problems, and to energize them, motivate them, assist them to be able to handle their own problems themselves, is no different than the psychology you take in to West Virginia or the South Bronx [in New York]. In the Peace Corps, one called this process "community development"; in the war against poverty, we called it "community action." [35]

While Shriver supported the idea of community action, he saw it as only one weapon in the antipoverty arsenal. "I knew," Shriver recalls, "that community action could not be the sole thing in the War on Poverty. . . . I still think the decision was correct, to make community action an essential part but not the whole of the War on Poverty." [36] Still, the Community Action Program is often called the heart of the War on Poverty. In the early stages of establishing his War on Poverty, Johnson thought back to his days as a teacher in the tiny poverty-stricken town of Cotulla, Texas. In Cotulla, poor parents became actively involved in their children's education by attending parent-teacher meetings. Johnson had discovered that programs worked bet-

ter when the people affected by them had a say in running them. So the concept of community action became a foundation of the War on Poverty.

Community Action

The plans for the programs that would fight poverty were laid out in the various sections, called titles, of the Economic Opportunity Act. The Community Action Program was established under Title II of the act. Under this title, local organizations known as community action agencies would be created to receive federal funds for fighting poverty in their own areas.

The actual operation of community action, for which independent local organizations received money directly from the

Sargent Shriver meets with a San Francisco community leader to enlist his support for the Community Action Program.

federal government, was a new concept and somewhat different than Johnson had envisioned. He had been thinking along the lines of a program that was part of President Franklin D. Roosevelt's New Deal during the Great Depression in the 1930s. The worst financial crisis in the nation's history, the Great Depression caused businesses to close, banks to fail, and unemployment to skyrocket. As a young man, Johnson had been the director in the state of Texas for a New Deal agency called the National Youth Administration (NYA). The NYA was a government agency that gave high school and college students grants for part-time and summer work, allowing them to stay in school and still bring in some badly needed additional income for their families. "I think President Johnson," Shriver recalled, "may have thought that the way community action was going to work was through local government. But, frankly, that never was my idea." [37]

Instead, Shriver saw the community action agencies as operating in the same manner as a local board of education. Just as a school board has the responsibility to speak out on behalf of students and teachers, the community action agencies would "speak out on behalf of poor people and the needs of poor people, whether they were needs for jobs or housing or health care—whatever those needs happened to be." [38] After existing as an overlooked minority in America, the people who were personally affected by poverty would at last have, in the words of Attorney General Robert F. Kennedy, "a real voice in their institutions." [39]

All across the country, local community action agencies set up neighborhood centers operating out of urban housing projects, storefronts, and other places in low income areas. In Oakland, California, for example, plans were made to open four neighborhood service centers. These centers were to provide such services as family counseling, legal advice, and health services to four neighborhoods where some eighty thousand poor people resided. From these centers, both professional and non-professional staff went out into the neighborhoods, often going house to house, to gather information on the needs, wants, and concerns of the local poor population and to inform the residents of the services that were available.

Money to fund centers such as those in Oakland was disbursed by the Office of Economic Opportunity and its use monitored by regional offices of the OEO. In fiscal 1966 the OEO approved over $650 million in CAP grants. The community action agencies helped disadvantaged people in their neighborhood to find jobs, get proper health care and nutrition information, obtain adequate housing, receive counseling for family problems, and learn how to better manage their money. In addition, they often provided emergency food and necessary community services to ward off starvation and malnutrition. According to one report, some typical cases included:

A landlord tried to evict a family on the basis of a lease that was changed after the tenants had signed it. The aide informed the family of their legal rights and at the same time pacified the landlord.

An aide helped an 81 year old in a housing project find other quarters, since the project was being demolished and the project manager was not even aware that she needed assistance.

A welfare recipient eager to become independent did not know that she could receive extra funds to go to school and additional money to pay a baby sitter from the Department of Social Services.

A family was threatened by PG&E [Pacific Gas and Electric] to have their service discontinued but the aide interceded and helped the husband obtain a job, persuading PG&E to wait another month.

An aide while going from house to house learned of a family just arrived from Texas with no funds or furniture. He enlisted the help of neighbors and local churches.

A mother in need of medical care and unable to speak English was persuaded by an aide to go to the hospital. The aide obtained a baby sitter and then personally took the mother to the hospital and interpreted for her. [40]

The Community Action Program was not without its problems and growing pains. Many local agencies were staffed by inexperienced workers and became burdened by problems in personnel, financial management, and administration. Originally conceived as an urban program, the CAP was criticized by some politicians for not doing enough for poverty-stricken rural areas. The mayors of some large cities feared the agencies would create politically militant groups in the high-poverty black ghettos, and state governors often felt left out as federal funds from the OEO bypassed their control. The highly charged political reaction to the OEO caused a *New York Times* reporter to comment, "Mr. Shriver and his Office of Economic Opportunity have inherited a thousand local political fights." [41]

About sixteen hundred community action agencies were in operation by 1968, covering more than two-thirds of America's counties. While the paid staffs of these organizations were helping the poor and disadvantaged, other Americans were giving their time freely as their part in the War on Poverty.

Volunteering with VISTA

Americans have always been volunteers. From the minutemen who helped gain freedom for the colonies, to the hospitals, churches, social agencies, and charities of today that rely on donated labor, volunteering has been an integral part of the American way of life. President Kennedy sought to bring that volunteer spirit to the task of helping underdeveloped nations with his Peace Corps. Under the Great Society, Lyndon Johnson took the same idea and employed it for dealing with poverty at home with a "domestic Peace Corps" known as VISTA—Volunteers in Service to

Lady Bird Visits VISTA

Lady Bird Johnson crisscrossed the country to promote her husband's Great Society programs. In February 1965 Lady Bird flew to St. Petersburg, Florida, to address the first graduating class of Volunteers in Service to America (VISTA). As Eric F. Goldman writes in his book, The Tragedy of Lyndon Johnson, *the commencement address was only the beginning.*

Then the real grind began: a visit to a remedial reading class, squeezed into one of the school desks for twenty minutes and leaving with an emphatic, "Y'all sure read that fast"; lunch in the steaming, clattering cafeteria of the VISTA school for cooking, seated between two of the VISTA graduates, a garrulous fledgling minister and an overwhelmed middle-aged spinster; the consumption, down to the last strangely colored glop, of student-cooked avocado stuffed with Gulf shrimp . . . a trip to the VISTA project in the nearby Negro slum where she went tramping over rocks and brambles to admire the work of the volunteers, ducked into trailers to tell the occupants how fine their improvements were, sat through another twenty-five minutes of a class, her lap full of azaleas and periwinkles pressed upon her; standing patiently for five minutes, waving back a Secret Service man, while a Negro tyke managed to make his battered camera work; a ten-minute change of clothing and the drive to the reception for the local powers at the new St. Petersburg Museum of Fine Arts . . . and at eight-thirty in the evening, after more than thirteen hours, back to the plane. Lady Bird Johnson settled in her seat, and now she looked a very tired woman indeed.

Lady Bird Johnson traveled the country to promote her husband's Great Society programs.

America. Sargent Shriver brought to VISTA the skills he used as head of the Peace Corps.

VISTA actually grew out of a Kennedy administration study group's idea for a domestic volunteer organization called the National Service Corps. While this idea never received the approval of Congress and was abandoned, VISTA took the same concept and made it a success. VISTA's mandate was to recruit and train volunteers to help alleviate need in the United States. By December 1964, less than four months after the Economic Opportunity Act became law, the first group of VISTA volunteers was formed. Although VISTA, like the Peace Corps, mainly targeted young college students and graduates in their recruiting, the first twenty volunteers ranged in age from eighteen to eighty-one. This initial volunteer group gathered at the White House to meet with Johnson, who welcomed them into a volunteer service that would be difficult but highly rewarding: "Your pay will be low; the conditions of your labor will often be difficult. But you will have the satisfaction of leading a great national effort and you will have the ultimate reward which comes to those who serve their fellow man."[42]

After receiving six weeks of training in Chapel Hill, North Carolina, the first VISTA volunteers were sent to work among the poor from Connecticut to California, in such disparate areas as big city slums, migrant worker camps, and depressed rural areas. Each volunteer committed to a one-year tour of duty in the region to which he or she was assigned.

The conditions the volunteers encountered upon arrival in their assigned areas often came as a shock. "Most of us didn't know what we were getting into," said one recruit. "The first thing that happened was that we found out how bad life can be. I guess that's the first step. I hope in a year we can find out what the second one is."[43]

Among its many accomplishments, VISTA established day care centers in communities of migrant workers and set up credit unions, agricultural cooperatives, and adult education programs in economically depressed areas ranging from Native American reservations to remote Alaskan towns. Many poor people received basic medical care for the first time. In the coal mining region of Appalachia, a debilitating disease called black lung killed and incapacitated thousands of miners each year, most of whom had no medical or disability insurance. VISTA helped obtain compensation for miners who became afflicted with the disease. VISTA volunteers also took part in community action agencies, educational projects, job training programs, and many other aspects of the War on Poverty. Peace Corps consultant Sam Brown writes: "At the heart of VISTA is a commitment to the welfare of one's fellow man, and its lifeblood, the dedication and compassion of the men and women who are at work on its behalf. . . . VISTA volunteers have demonstrated the true spirit and the substance of brotherhood. They have made a difference in many lives, bringing help and hope to those locked in the wrenching vise of poverty and despair."[44]

Training for Work

One of the problems that plagued young people living in disadvantaged areas of the United States in the 1960s was that many lacked the education and practical skills needed to acquire and hold a job. Without gainful employment, drug use and petty crime among poor juveniles flourished. Such persons had little hope of escaping decaying urban ghettos or impoverished rural areas, resulting in a cycle of poverty from one generation to the next.

One aspect of the Great Society was specifically aimed at the problem of widespread unemployment among America's youth due to lack of adequate education. But even before Johnson launched his War on Poverty, this problem was being examined. During the Kennedy administration,

a study was made by the Task Force on Manpower Utilization to determine why the rejection rate of the Selective Service System was so high. The task force's report, entitled *One-Third of a Nation*, revealed that one out of three eighteen-year-olds who were drafted into the armed forces did not meet the physical or mental requirements for military service. Most of the rejected young men, the study found, came from underprivileged households. If these youths were not educated well enough to be accepted by the military, their chances of success in the civilian business world would likewise be severely limited.

Further studies made by Johnson's War on Poverty found that almost three-quarters of a million youths dropped out

Job Corps participants study during a reading class. The Job Corps was a residential program offering educational instruction, work experience, and job training.

of school annually. In addition, it was discovered that the unemployment rate among urban youth was nearly 50 percent. Obviously, something had to be done to prepare these young people to become employed and productive members of society.

A Residential Program for Youths

In early 1964, as Sargent Shriver and his task force discussed the direction the War on Poverty should take, an idea arose for helping high school dropouts. The idea included a form of "urban boarding schools" for young men whose home environment made getting a proper education extremely difficult if not impossi-

ble. (Young women were not initially considered for this program, known as the Job Corps, since they tended to stay in school longer and had an easier time finding jobs after graduation.) "It was important," Shriver said, " . . . to put [the young men] in a different environment, 24 hours a day, 365 days a year . . . expose them to a new culture . . . of work . . . of discipline . . . of personal responsibility."[45] Abandoned military bases were suggested as facilities for these boarding schools. A lengthy debate ensued over the name of the new program, but it was eventually ended when Shriver finally declared, "Nuts, let's call it the Job Corps. That's what these kids are really interested in—a job."[46]

One feature of the program was immediately controversial: a proposal that the

Department of Defense run it. This idea conflicted with the long-established principle of keeping a separation between the military and civilian worlds. Questions arose about the appropriateness of Defense Department control over a civilian educational program like the Job Corps. Congress opposed military involvement in a social program, and thus would surely have rejected the Job Corps program. Ultimately the military's role in the Job Corps was reduced to supplying administrative and logistical services.

The Department of Defense was not the only group with ideas on how the Job Corps should be designed. Conservationists wanted to make sure that Job Corps enrollees would be put to work in national parks and other public areas to help husband America's natural resources. This was not a new idea; it went back to the days of the Great Depression. As part of his New Deal, President Franklin Roosevelt had formed the Civilian Conservation Corps (CCC), an agency that put young men to work on outdoor conservation projects such as building roads and planting trees. Johnson's poverty planners were wary of such a scheme, fearing that the conservationists were more concerned with simply getting free labor out of Job Corps youths rather than preparing them for future jobs. Shriver commented that the Job Corps was designed to "help kids, not trees." [47] But the conservation lobby was influential with Congress, and a deal was made to allow up to 40 percent of Job Corps enrollees to work at conservation camps.

The Job Corps Program

As it was finally established, the Job Corps included both the conservationists' concept of outdoor work camps and the urban boarding school idea. Sociology professor Sar Levitan describes the two types of Job Corps centers as "rural centers where youths with acute educational difficulties would receive basic educational instruction and work experience on conservation projects; and urban centers where individuals with at least a sixth-grade educational level would receive vocational training." [48] The urban centers would be operated by universities or nonprofit organizations and by large private corporations such as RCA, IBM, and Westinghouse. Operation of the conservation camps would be the joint responsibility of the U.S. Departments of Agriculture and Interior. The urban centers were larger, averaging from 1,500 to 3,000 enrollees. The rural camps generally enrolled from 100 to 250 Job Corps recruits.

The Job Corps was designed for young men aged sixteen to twenty-one who were not in school and lived in decaying and underprivileged neighborhoods. The male-only composition of the Job Corps was challenged by Congresswoman Edith Green. She argued that many young women, especially those who came from poor backgrounds, were likely to have children who would remain stuck in the cycle of poverty. As a result, the Job Corps planners agreed that women would be included in the program. Since it was determined that young women could not perform the heavy physical labor of the conservation camps, a third type of center, located mostly in urban areas, was created for Job Corps women. Although these women's centers were initially kept small in size, Congress later mandated that women fill 50 percent of Job Corps openings.

In March 1964 President Johnson described the basic elements of what he envisioned as the War on Poverty's training program for at-risk youth. "A new national Job Corps," he wrote, "will build toward an enlistment of 100,000 young men. They will be drawn from those whose background, health and education make them least fit for useful work. Those who volunteer will enter more than one hundred Camps and Centers around the country."[49] Johnson's estimate of one hundred thousand participants would prove to be overly optimistic; after two years of operation the Job Corps program could accommodate just forty-three thousand enrollees.

In the fall of 1964 Shriver recruited Otis Singletary to head up the new agency. Singletary, chancellor of the University of North Carolina, took a one-year leave of absence to accept the position. The choice of an educator as head of the Job Corps emphasized the educational component of the agency. "Shriver felt all along that the

Job Corps recruits in North Carolina make their way to school and to work. President Johnson originally envisioned a corps offering services to one hundred thousand participants.

Arrival at Catoctin Mountain

For many Job Corps youth, their stay at the training camp at Catoctin Mountain, Maryland, was their first time away from home. To anyone observing these poor youths as they arrived at the camp, the ravages of poverty could be clearly observed. The following passage from a 1965 article about the opening of the Catoctin Mountain camp is taken from the February 27, 1995, issue of Time *magazine:*

The youths at Catoctin Mountain are a pathetic lot. One is Robert Collier, 16, a pale, skinny boy from Big Stone Gap, Va., who had hardly got settled in camp when he had to have 14 teeth extracted. Asked when he had last been to a dentist, he replied, "I ain't never been." Another is Ray Martin, 18, who hails from "a holler" near Isom, Ky. At six, Martin was gathering coal in an abandoned mine shaft to provide the family's fuel. When Martin left home to travel to Catoctin Mountain, his mother told him, "Don't come back, son. There's nothing for you here."

program had to have prestige in the eyes of the public," explains Vernon R. Alden, who helped direct the planning of the Job Corps. "He could have had a school superintendent or a school board member, but I think that Sarge really wanted to give the program a little bit of distinction by saying a university president would run it."[50]

Opening the Camps

Begun with an initial federal funding of $190 million, the Job Corps provided job training for high risk youth, those least likely to succeed. They were poor, many had drug habits, or had turned to crime as a way of making a little money. Most enrollees came to the Job Corps program with only a ninth grade education; many had difficulty in reading or doing simple arithmetic. More

than 60 percent came from broken homes, or homes where the head of the family was unemployed. To recruit these youths, Job Corps workers relied on local churches, schools, Boys Clubs, and other agencies to get the word out. In addition, Job Corps packets were distributed by the U.S. Employment Service, with reply postcards enclosed. The recruiting process was an overwhelming success, and by January 1965 some fifteen thousand Job Corps applications a week were being received. By the middle of 1965 about ten thousand young men had been recruited into the Job Corps, even though many of the centers had yet to be completed.

Preparations for opening the first Job Corps center began in January 1965 when a busload of thirty young men pulled up to a site called Camp Round Meadow in Catoctin Mountain Park, Maryland. Upon stepping off the bus, seventeen-year-old Chester Maggard and his fellow recruits looked in despair at their new surroundings:

Chester immediately wondered how far the nearest town was; Catoctin looked as if it was really out in the sticks. Another glanced around and asked one of the men standing nearby where the fences were; he had expected the center to be closed in somehow, like a concentration camp. But mostly what they saw was snow and more snow. It was a cold beginning.[51]

But as cold as it was that January day, these young men were about to be given a chance at a new life. Christopher Weeks described these first Job Corps volunteers:

Drawn from the depths of poverty-stricken Appalachia and the ghettos of Baltimore, these men were the first Job Corps recruits entering the first Job Corps center. . . . The hopes of these young men ran high. They had been told about a new program—nationwide in scope—which would give them the education and job training they wanted in order to be a success in life. They would get this in a place called a Job Corps center where they would live for six months or more with other boys. At the center they would get three square meals a day, learn how to use power tools and heavy equipment like bulldozers and dump trucks. . . . At the end of their training, the Job Corps would help them find a job and pay them a mustering out allowance to tide them over until the first paycheck came in.[52]

Chester Maggard's group and other young recruits spent several months readying the camp for use by building sidewalks, doing landscaping, and performing other chores. The new recruits "knew they had been selected because they were dropouts with little future; to most of them this was a painfully clear fact of life—at least until the Job Corps recruiter came along. Now they were in the Job Corps. One of them quickly made up a motto for the new program; his proposal was 'Your Last Chance.'"[53]

On February 27 the camp was officially dedicated with 85 job corpsmen and 150 guests in attendance. Activities at the camp continued year-round. In the winter months, the youths spent half of each day working and half in classes. During the summers, full days of work alternated with days of classroom learning. Young workers repaired trails in the park, built picnic tables, and created hundreds of signs for Catoctin Mountain Park and other national parks in the vicinity. Early in March 1965 President Johnson visited the Job Corps site at Catoctin, which was located not far from Camp David, the Maryland presidential retreat.

Less than two months after the Catoctin camp began its operation, the first women's

Job Corps center was opened in Cleveland, Ohio. During the first year of the program eighty-seven Job Corps centers had been opened, providing training for nearly seventeen thousand young men and women. The average annual cost to train, house, clothe, and feed one male Job Corps enrollee was about eighty-seven hundred dollars; for females it was more than ninety-six hundred dollars. By 1966 there were about twelve urban men's centers, more than eighty conservation camps, and seventeen women's centers in operation.

Urban and Rural

Job Corps recruits came from all over the United States, from large cities to sparsely populated rural areas. Sometimes the

During their stay, Job Corpsmen like these learned to perform a variety of functions, from typing correspondence to operating heavy machinery.

combination of urban and rural youth in one center became a problem for the Job Corps. Christopher Weeks describes a difficult situation:

What you had in many Job Corps centers was a mixture of big, black, urban, street-smart kids with physically small, underfed white kids from rural poverty, many of whom had hardly seen a black before. It was a pretty explosive mixture. Until you could see the kids come off the buses—and you could count the rural kids as they got off the buses, because they would be four or five, six inches shorter than the rest, and their weight would be thirty, forty, fifty pounds lighter. Half their teeth would be gone. They would be obviously victims of malnutrition. Their faces would be covered with poor skin conditions, the whole works. You put a bunch of kids like that together with a bunch of street-smart urban kids, and you've got a tough problem. [54]

Choosing the Poor

During the development stage of the Job Corps, a decision had to be made: which of the many unemployed poor deserved to get the first places in the Job Corps camps? Ann Oppenheimer Hamilton, who worked for the Bureau of the Budget in 1964, describes the debate in Launching the War on Poverty: An Oral History, *by Michael L. Gillette.*

The issue was how to tackle the really hard-core unemployed, almost untrainable young people, and get them back on the ladder of economic development, as the expression was. How to get them on the bottom rung, and did we try for that? Did we try to tackle the problem of real hard-core poverty, or did we take the easier cases who just happened to be suffering from a much more superficial combination of adverse circumstances and give them the little boost that was necessary: the ones that were already motivated, willing, and *only* poor? . . .

[Taking the latter group] was a philosophy that tended to prevail, for very obvious reasons. You don't go for the most difficult cases first, because your chances of failure—and therefore failure of the whole program—are greater. You go for areas where your chances of success are greater and hope that once you've gotten the program established, you learn enough and develop enough of a basis of support to go for the harder cases later.

The problems that arose during the first years of the Job Corps were many. Job Corps centers were plagued by a high dropout rate, as much as 20 percent in the first thirty days of a recruit's stay. Many enrollees remained in the program only a few weeks before becoming homesick and leaving the camps. Isolated acts of violence, both within the camps and in the surrounding communities, spawned a great deal of negative press that put the program in an unfavorable light. The relatively high cost per Job Corps volunteer caused Congress to adopt an annual limit of seventy-five hundred dollars per recruit in 1967. The following year that amount was reduced to sixty-nine hundred dollars.

Race also played a part in the planning of at least one Job Corps facility. One local community in Virginia objected to the planned opening of a Job Corps center, fearing an influx of African Americans from northern ghettos. Shriver attempted to allay the community's fears:

Every member of the Job Corps will be carefully screened and will be the kind of American who could be welcomed anywhere in the United States. Job Corps camps will not be composed of all Negroes, or of all Spanish-speaking Americans, or of all rural white people, or of all anything else. . . . [Critics are] grossly misinformed about the Job Corps. There is no substance to their worries. [55]

In spite of Shriver's efforts, the Job Corps center was never built.

The longer young people stayed in the Job Corps, the better their chances of achieving success. An independent study found that 75 percent of youth who stayed in the Job Corps for more than six months felt they were better off than before. The study also found that:

There is clear evidence that a successful stay in the Job Corps can improve a youth's chances. The graduates and those in centers over six months have not only improved their employment situation and their pay rate more than the other groups, but they also sensed this improvement. Whether these groups will maintain their advantage in the future is a question that, at this point, cannot be answered. [56]

While the Job Corps took at-risk youth away from home to provide the education and jobs they needed, other young people were given help in their own neighborhoods.

Neighborhood Youth Corps

Under the Economic Opportunity Act, OEO director Sargent Shriver could choose to delegate the operation of War on Poverty programs to other government agencies. He gave the task of supervising another youth employment program, the Neighborhood Youth Corps (NYC), to the U.S. Department of Labor. The purpose of the NYC, as described by the man who initiated the idea, Senator Hubert Humphrey, was "to put idle youth to work constructively and, in some cases, to help prevent high school dropouts by providing part-time work. This program . . . would provide many needed community jobs." [57] With a budget of $130 million for its first year of operation, the NYC provided work experience for unemployed young men and women ranging in age from fourteen to twenty-one. In contrast to the Job Corps, which separated enrollees from their neighborhoods, the NYC worked with disadvantaged young people within their own communities. It emphasized paid work experience rather than training, concentrating on keeping juveniles in school (or providing dropouts the opportunity to return to school) while allowing them to earn extra income needed by their families.

Initially there were two components to the Neighborhood Youth Corps program. The first component provided part-time employment for young people who were still in school; the second one arranged full-time jobs for those who had already dropped out and were unemployed. Eventually a third component, a summer employment program, provided jobs for both groups. Those enrolled in the in-school program worked a maximum of fifteen hours a week, and those in the out-of-school program worked about thirty-two hours weekly. Summer employment averaged twenty-eight hours a week. Although overseen by the Department of Labor, the actual administration of the NYC program was performed by nonprofit organizations and public agencies such as community action agencies, hospitals, public libraries, and schools. These sponsors paid 10 percent of the cost of running the NYC program.

Putting Skills to Work

Participants in the Neighborhood Youth Corps learned the basic job skills that they would need to become useful employees, such as taking direction from a supervisor and how to work together in task-related groups. "One of the greatest benefits for enrollees," commented Robert Schrank, a noted authority on youth employment, "is learning how to navigate through the bureaucracies. . . . This is what many of the enrollees don't know. Being in the Neighborhood Youth Corps gives them a chance to learn. . . . That's one of the things we mean by employability." [58]

The NYC participants then put their skills to work. Those in the in-school program performed a variety of jobs in their schools, including work as custodians, teachers' aides, library workers, and carrying out other clerical duties. In the out-of-school program, enrollees worked in hospitals, public libraries, and other public institutions. In general, young women did clerical work while the young men were given the more physical jobs such as maintenance and custodial work. An early problem arose concerning the type of work offered the NYC enrollees by the sponsoring organizations. Since the sponsors paid only 10 percent of the cost for employing NYC workers, they were get-

Senator Hubert Humphrey conceived the Neighborhood Youth Corps to provide jobs for America's youth.

ting what amounted to almost free labor. They often matched it with trivial jobs instead of meaningful work and job experience that would be useful in future employment. This jeopardized the goals of the NYC.

Evaluating the Program

Did the Neighborhood Youth Corps fulfill its goals? Opinions differed. Of the efforts of the in-school program to deter dropping out, one study declared that the NYC had "a decisive effect on helping to curb the increase of youth dropping out of school," while another study noted "no significant change." [59] Another report suggested that the NYC summer program "is not an effective vehicle for attracting young dropouts back to school." [60] Still, the Neighborhood Youth Corps succeeded in preparing many of their enrollees, especially young women, for jobs. And many of them later expressed positive reactions to their NYC experience. Unfortunately, many NYC participants remained under the poverty level even after completing the program and would need further education to escape the ranks of the poor.

Education

As a former teacher, Lyndon Johnson knew the importance of an education for all young people, but especially what it meant for underprivileged youth. In Cotulla, Texas, where he taught the children of Mexican American farmworkers, Johnson saw education as an escape route for poverty-stricken children from a bleak future of backbreaking work with minimal rewards. One of the most important and successful programs of Johnson's Great Society dealt with the education of preschool-aged children. But at the outset of the War on Poverty, the program received scant mention and no mandate in the Economic Opportunity Act.

Children at Risk

In its first year, the centerpiece of Lyndon Johnson's War on Poverty—the Community Action Program—had a problem: it was finding it difficult to spend all its money. For its first year of operation the CAP had been allocated $300 million by Congress. But not enough cities had taken part in the program, and by the middle of 1964 only $26 million of CAP's appropriation had been spent. Sargent Shriver, director of the Office of Economic Opportunity (OEO), knew how things worked in Washington: if you do not spend the money Congress gives you, the next time appropriations come around you are sure to get less. He needed to find a way to spend the surplus CAP funds. In the fall of 1964 Shriver met with OEO researchers and asked them to investigate how best to use the excess CAP money to combat poverty. Included in the report of their investigation was a chart illustrating that children made up almost half of America's poor. Shriver was astonished. "It was clear," he said, "that it was foolish to talk about a 'total war against poverty' . . . if you were doing nothing about children." [61]

The Importance of Education

As a former teacher, Lyndon Johnson was a firm believer in the necessity of a good education for everyone, so naturally education played a large role in the War on Poverty. In this passage from The Vantage Point, *Johnson writes about the importance of educating even the youngest Americans.*

Experts tell us that most of a child's full potential is achieved before he reaches school age. Half his eventual capacity has been established by the age of four. By the time he is six, two-thirds of his adult intelligence has been formed. How do such findings square with the notion that the "education" of a child does not begin until he is six? The Head Start program we inaugurated led the way in the application of these discoveries to the classroom. Focused on culturally deprived children, Head Start was responsible for calling attention to several incredible facts. Almost half the children we reached with this program the first year came from homes that had no toys, books, magazines, crayons, paints, or even paper. Some of those children, particularly those from city slums, could not recognize pictures of animals from the zoo. The only animal they all knew immediately was a rat. One little black girl literally did not know what the word "beautiful" meant and she was overjoyed to discover its meaning as she watched herself in a mirror, trying on her teacher's hat.

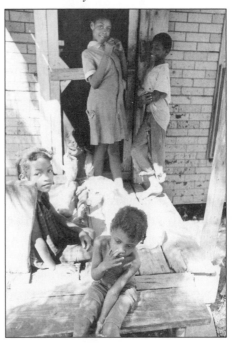

Providing poor children with a quality education was an integral part of the War on Poverty.

Shriver was sensitive to the need for education, especially among disadvantaged children. He had been appointed to the Chicago Board of Education in 1954, becoming its president the next year. During his tenure he was instrumental in securing board approval of a program for improving the academic standards for Chicago high schools, as well as for increasing teachers' salaries and raising overall enrollment in the schools. He also began developing an idea to prepare underprivileged preschool children for entry into school, because he had seen firsthand "how the cards are stacked against kids in the slums in a huge number of ways." [62] Both Shriver and his wife Eunice, sister of President John F. Kennedy, had long been involved with the Joseph P. Kennedy Jr. Foundation, an organization established to confront the problems of mental retardation. The results of a research project, begun in 1962 and funded in part by the foundation, intrigued Shriver. This project, entitled the Early Training Project, provided educational experiences for preschool children whose impoverished home environment had retarded their intellectual capacity. It discovered that if intervention began early enough, the intelligence quotient (IQ) of disadvantaged preschool children could actually be raised. "Being of an era," Shriver recalled, "when we thought you were born with an IQ just as you were born with blue eyes, that fact really impressed me and stuck in my head." [63] The Early Training Project would become the inspiration for Shriver's own preschool education effort in the War on Poverty.

Creating Head Start

Shriver knew that young, at-risk children had to be one of the most important groups to benefit from the War on Poverty. In December 1964 he proposed the formation of a planning committee to take a look at ways of implementing an early education program. Robert Cooke, chief pediatrician at Johns Hopkins Hospital and the Shriver family pediatrician, was asked to head up the committee. "My contribution was getting the right people," [64] Cooke said. Whereas Shriver had been thinking along the lines of an educational program only, as a doctor Cooke also made sure that the project would include medical care as one of its key elements. Thus the planning committee included physicians as well as psychologists, educators, and child development specialists, for a total of fourteen members.

The committee had six weeks to hammer out a proposal for the program. Meeting eight times during that time, the members discussed such topics as better health care as a prerequisite for improved school performance, parent involvement in the child's education, and provisions for activities that would allow children to expect success in their learning. Another task for the committee was to come up with a name for the project. During the meetings several names were tossed around, but the name Head Start seemed to have the positive, uplifting quality Shriver was looking for. "Everyone's been in some kind of a foot race," Shriver recalled, "where one group, by reason of

Preschoolers in a California Head Start program listen to an educational tape. Head Start offered education and health services to at-risk children.

a handicap, is given a head start. It was a facile phrase, and it actually did represent what were trying to give these kids—a running head start."[65]

By February 1965 the committee had settled on the elements that would make up the project and put them in a memo to Shriver. Entitled "Recommendations for a Head Start Program by a Panel of Experts," the report states:

It is clear that successful programs of this type must be comprehensive, involving activities generally associated with the fields of health, social services and education. Similarly, it is

clear that the program must focus on the child and the parent, and that these activities need to be carefully integrated with programs for the school years.[66]

The committee had not yet determined just how much Head Start was going to cost. Shriver asked Jule Sugarman, the executive secretary of the committee, to figure out the cost of the program for each child it helped. When Sugarman said he would look into the matter Shriver replied, "Fine, you have an hour!"[67] Over a quick lunch, Sugarman and a colleague fixed the cost per child of

Head Start at $180. As it turned out, this hasty estimate was remarkably accurate: the average cost per child of the first summer's program was $186.

Teaching the Children

The committee decided that rather than beginning on a limited trial basis, the Head Start program would be launched nationwide. It was a bold plan, but it turned out to be the correct one. If Head Start had started small, it would not have been strong enough to survive its early growing pains. On February 12, 1965, Lady Bird Johnson, who became the honorary chairman of Head Start, held a tea at the White House to announce the beginning of the Head Start program. Some four hundred people attended the event as the First Lady talked about Head Start as a way to reach children

Lady Bird Johnson (right) speaks at a Head Start luncheon in 1965. The First Lady announced the program's launch in February of that year.

"lost in a gray world of poverty and neglect, and lead them into the human family." [68] The resulting national media coverage, appearing mostly in the society pages of newspapers, led some two hundred thousand people to become Head Start volunteers.

To make sure that the program reached the neediest children, interns traveled to the poorest counties in the nation to help local volunteers complete applications for Head Start grants. In all, thirty-three hundred applications were filed for the first summer Head Start program, covering three-quarters of the nation's three hundred counties hit hardest by poverty. Local Head Start centers were set up in churches, synagogues, community centers, lodge meeting halls, anywhere space could be found. Head Start began as an eight-week program in the summer of 1965 and enrolled children from three to six years old. Most of them were desperately in need of educational enrichment in their lives. According to one observer, many of the children in the Head Start program "had never opened a book or touched a pencil, had never eaten an apple or used a knife and fork, and, in some cases, had never talked because no one had talked to them. Many did not recognize colors and could not identify everyday objects." [69] The children sang songs, drew pictures, and were taught skills that they would need upon entering school. They were given medical and dental examinations, some for the first time in their lives, and they received nutritious meals of the kind their parents could not afford to give them.

By the end of the summer half a million children had been enrolled in the Head Start program and somewhere between $50 million and $70 million had been spent. In 1966 the Head Start program began operating year-round. One man recalls his Head Start days of some thirty years before:

> The whole neighborhood was there. It was very community oriented. You knew everybody. You not only played with them at school, but you saw them in the street. Even the teachers were from the neighborhood. And if they didn't catch up with you at school, you knew they'd catch up with you at church or somewhere.
>
> One day was about four or five hours, I think. . . . The classes were small. Each teacher helped you individually. When I got to first grade I felt comfortable. [Head Start] was good preparation. Even if you didn't know your ABCs and 1-2-3s, you had started on them. Everything was familiar and you were in a learning mode. . . .
>
> [Head Start] also gave us a sense of community. From the beginning, we learned that school wasn't a competition. And except for sports, it wasn't a competition. We helped each other out all the way through. [70]

While Head Start was helping prepare preschoolers for their grammar school years, another program was providing assistance to students at the other end of the educational spectrum.

Upward Bound

Going to college and succeeding at college-level studies is the ultimate goal for many high school students. But the environment at a college or university is very different from what most high school students have experienced. For low-income families especially, the advantages of a college education can often seem out of reach. The Upward Bound program was created to assist students from such families to achieve their higher-education goals.

In 1963 the American Council on Education instituted several precollege educational programs in African American colleges, aimed primarily at preparing disadvantaged black high school students for college. Soon other colleges and universities began similar programs, and when the Economic Opportunity Act was passed in 1964, several of these institutions applied for funding from the Office of Economic Opportunity. In 1965 a pilot program of eighteen projects was launched. Theodore M. Berry, assistant director of the OEO's Community Action Programs from 1965 to 1969, recalls:

Most of these institutions were Negro, or black, institutions. There were some colleges up in the northeast. But that first year's experience validated our theory, so much so that in the next year we were able to . . . [open] the eyes and the minds and the interest of the staid college institutions . . . in terms of motivating, helping poor youth who had low academic achievement to begin to get a sense of their own capability [and developing] the interest of these institutions in them. [71]

These initial efforts led to a nationwide rollout of the Upward Bound program in 1966. More than two hundred colleges and universities received grants, allowing them to serve over twenty thousand students that year.

Students selected for the Upward Bound program usually were those whose high school performance showed a high probability of success if they attended college. This somewhat exclusive selection process engendered some initial complaints. Critics said that in choosing the "best" students rather than students from the entire universe of poor young people, the impact on poverty would be negligible, since those chosen would probably have succeeded in college anyway. Despite its critics, Upward Bound was a success. Studies indicated that 60 to 70 percent of Upward Bound students went on to attend college, with one-third of them completing a full four year course of studies.

The students spent six to eight weeks on a college campus, doing academic work designed to prepare them for the rigors of college. They lived in dormitories, which gave them a feel for what it was like to be a residential student on a college campus. Regular students at the colleges lived with the Upward Bound students, tutoring them in various academic subjects and providing counseling when needed. Medical,

President Johnson signs the Higher Education Act in November 1965. The law provided money to fund Upward Bound, a program to help poor students obtain a college education.

dental, and psychological care were also given to those students who needed them. Attendance at follow-up sessions held on evenings and weekends after the summer session was over numbered 95 percent of the summer students. By 1969 some fifty-five thousand students had participated in the Upward Bound program.

Elementary and Secondary Education Act

By the 1960s schools in America were under pressure to increase the efficiency and quality of their teaching. The large number of children born after World War II had reached school age and their num-

bers strained both educational facilities and teachers. With the launch of the first artificial satellite by the Soviet Union, cries for increased education in science and technology were being heard across the nation. As might be expected, schools in the poorest areas needed the most help. According to the president of the teachers' association in Philadelphia, poor children there attended schools "where plaster drops from the ceiling; broke[n] windows go unfixed; adequate toilet facilities are nonexistent; and broken and faulty heaters endanger their health."[72] What the schools needed was financial aid from the federal government, and polls showed that three-quarters of the

American public agreed. A bill for federal aid to schools was drafted and sent to Congress for debate.

Questions immediately arose. Should the federal government be in the business of funding education in America, or was that a responsibility of the states? Would the bill lead to federal control of the schools, which were traditionally governed by local school boards? Should private schools receive funding? And what about religious schools, given the constitutional mandate of separation between church and state? A Republican representative called the bill "one of the most dangerous mea-

sures that has come before us in my time."[73] But the idea had its supporters in Congress and during congressional debates the major problems were eventually overcome. The constitutional question was resolved by the "child benefit theory," which asserted that financial aid was appropriate because the ultimate recipients were the students themselves, regardless of the type of school they attended.

The result was the Elementary and Secondary Education Act (ESEA), which Johnson signed into law on April 11, 1965. The bill, Johnson said, "represents a major new commitment of the Federal

President Johnson signs the Elementary and Secondary Education Act in April 1965. The act provided $1 billion to improve educational services in America's poorest areas.

Government to quality and equality in the schooling that we offer our young people. . . . By passing this bill, we bridge the gap between helplessness and hope for more than 5 million educationally deprived children." [74] The ESEA became the most important and far-reaching element of the War on Poverty's educational program. The principle behind the act was that poor children needed more educational assistance than children from affluent homes. Title I of the ESEA allocated $1 billion in federal funding to improve the education of children attending schools in inner-city slums and poverty-stricken rural areas. Other titles, or sections, of the act provided for the purchase of textbooks, called for the creation of innovative supplemental educational centers, funded educational research, and prevented the federal government from exercising control over local school districts.

Adult Basic Education

Education is important not only to children, but to adults as well. And the Great Society was prepared to help adults also reach their educational goals.

Without the ability to read, write, and do basic arithmetic, a person's ability to get and keep a job is severely limited. And without a job there is little hope for escape from poverty. In 1960 there were about 4 million teenagers and adults (persons fourteen years old and older) in the United States who were considered illiterate. The War on Poverty recognized the problem and set about to increase the opportunity for adults to receive the basic educational tools they would need to become working members of society.

Adult education under Johnson's Great Society began with the Economic Opportunity Act in 1964, which mandated the states to establish the means for adult education programs. Two years later the Adult Education Act of 1966 made funds available to the states to begin educational programs for men and women eighteen years of age and older who were hindered in obtaining a job by the lack of reading and writing skills. States used federal grants from the Office of Economic Opportunity to create curricula specifically tailored to the needs of adults, to hire teachers, and to administer adult classes at local public elementary or secondary schools. Classes were also created to serve adults for whom English was a second language. Each state received at least $50,000 in federal grants from a first year total expenditure of more than $18 million.

Johnson later recalled his satisfaction "in the thought that thousands of children got a head start because of our combined efforts, and that many older people learned to read and write for the first time." [75] As important as the War on Poverty's efforts were for improving education in America, helping the poor gain access to better health care was also a priority for Johnson's Great Society.

Chapter 6

Health and Legal Services

Lack of education, decent housing, and a well-paying job are all associated with poverty. So is lack of health care. The problems of inadequate health care appear with distressing regularity. These include the parent afflicted by a chronic illness that keeps him or her from holding onto a job; the child stricken with a disease that could have been prevented by proper vaccination; the elderly person on a fixed income who must choose between buying food or medicine. The War on Poverty attempted to address these conditions with two types of programs: neighborhood health centers and the financing of health care for the elderly and poor.

Neighborhood Health Centers

By 1965 the Office of Economic Opportunity (OEO) had become concerned about the availability, or rather the lack, of proper health care for the poor. Few poor people could afford health insurance on their own and low-paying jobs rarely provided such benefits, so illnesses or chronic medical conditions often went untreated. When things got too bad, the poor often went to the emergency room of their local hospital, which became a sort of clinic for the disadvantaged. But there just were not enough doctors and other health care workers to properly minister to the needs of the poor. Under the OEO the Office of

Comprehensive Health Services was created to remedy this situation by establishing neighborhood health centers. According to an agency report, the proposed centers would offer "virtually all non-hospital medical services for all members of a family within one centrally located facility in a designated poverty community. The . . . services . . . include preventive medicine, diagnosis, treatment, dental care, drugs and appliances, mental health services, family planning, and health education." [76] But the neighborhood health centers would not only provide health care; they would also endeavor to connect their patients with various community service organizations to help them deal with other problems of poverty.

The neighborhood health center project began in 1965 with a $2 million grant to open two demonstration projects as a test of the local health center concept. The next year ten grants were awarded, and in 1967 federal funding increased to more than $50 million with thirty-nine grants. These grants went to such organizations as hospitals, medical schools, community action agencies, group medical practices, and others who would use the funds for improving health care for the poor in their local neighborhoods. An integral part of the program was the involvement of people from the communities in which the centers were established. As one health policy specialist notes, this process "called for new attitudes on the part not only of consumers, but also health

An elderly patient meets with President Johnson. In 1965 the Johnson administration established neighborhood clinics across the country to provide health care to poor families.

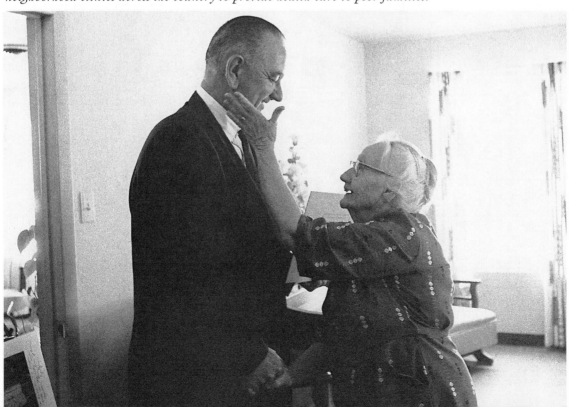

An Honor for Truman

Harry S. Truman, who was president of the United States from 1945 to 1953, was an advocate of government health insurance for the elderly. The Medicare bill was finally signed into law by Lyndon Johnson in 1965, but the signing did not take place in Washington, as Johnson relates in his memoirs, The Vantage Point.

I had a special reason for wanting to sign Medicare into law before the end of July. It would mean an extra $30 million in benefits to the aged. I had a particular place in mind for the signing. On July 27 I called President Truman and told him I wanted to come out and have a special visit with him. On July 30 I traveled to Independence, Missouri, to sign the bill in Mr. Truman's presence in the library that bears his name. He had started it all, so many years before. I wanted him to know that America remembered. It was a proud day for all of us, and President Truman said that no single honor ever paid him had touched him more deeply.

President Lyndon Johnson signs the Medicare bill in 1965 while former president Harry Truman looks on.

professionals and program managers."[77] Local residents served on advisory boards and worked in the centers in entry-level positions, giving them valuable job experience.

Health care was provided free to those with incomes below the poverty level, and on a sliding scale for others. The OEO recommended that the centers not only treat disease but offer such services as health screening, immunizations, drug abuse prevention, family planning, dental care, rehabilitation assistance, environmental services such as rodent control, and in-home medical care. In 1967 the government called for the establishment by 1973 of one thousand neighborhood health centers, which were expected to serve some 25 million poor people. As with many of Johnson's poverty programs that were rushed into operation, the health centers experienced growing pains. Problems with inadequate supplies and unpaid bills plagued some of the centers. There also were concerns about the quality of care provided by the centers, but studies eventually determined that the quality of their services was "generally equal to, and in some cases superior to that of other established providers of health care."[78]

While the Office of Economic Opportunity was working on getting health care to Americans living in poverty, another group of citizens with their own special health needs was waiting for the government to recognize their needs as well.

Health Care for the Elderly

When Lyndon Johnson won by a landslide in the 1964 presidential election, the mo-

mentum for his Great Society increased. One area the president had an interest in was health care. When Congress convened in 1965, Johnson made his desires clear: "Unless we do better," he said, "two-thirds of all Americans now living will suffer or die from cancer, heart disease, or stroke. . . . [The answer is] to assure the availability of and accessibility to the best health care for all Americans regardless of age, geography, or economic status."[79]

Providing health care for the underprivileged and elderly was seen as an admirable undertaking, but proposals for how to accomplish this brought strong opposition. Legislation to create a health plan that would provide care for all Americans, regardless of their ability to pay, had been proposed by President Harry S. Truman in 1948. Under such a system, which was sometimes called socialized medicine by its critics, the government would provide free or low-cost health services for all Americans, and put the burden of paying for it on the taxpayers. The plan was defeated by a Republican-dominated Congress. Conservatives at the time disliked the idea and worked hard to oppose any effort to enact such legislation. But by the time Lyndon Johnson was in the White House, a Democratic-controlled Congress was more inclined to favor a nationwide health plan.

The need was certainly there: forty-four percent of the elderly had no medical insurance coverage in 1964, and more than one-third of all Americans over age sixty-five lived under the poverty line. But such statistics simply relate dry information. For

Johnson the heart of the matter was conveyed in letters such as this one sent to him by a woman in Washington:

> I have never done anything as daring as writing to the top man of our wonderful nation. But things are getting awfully rough at our house, so I thought I would start at the top, as we are already at the bottom. . . . You see, my husband for almost 46 years has had several strokes. . . . We had both worked and bought [savings] bonds and were doing okay, when my husband became ill. Now the bonds are gone. I can't borrow because we can't repay a loan. We have two very fine children, but both have families and homes to keep up too, so we can't expect any financial aid from them.[80]

For another senior, a simple phrase summed it up: "I just don't want to be a burden to anyone."[81]

Johnson urged the senators and representatives to pass a health care bill for the elderly. Upon introducing such a bill, Congressman Cecil King said, "We can no longer permit hospital costs—or fear of hospital costs—to deprive our elderly citizens of the security and peace of mind that should be their due after a lifetime of work."[82] Despite the growing realization that a senior health care program was needed, Johnson's bill, like Truman's, met opposition, but mostly from outside Congress. The American Medical Association (AMA), for example, was against any federal inter-ference in health matters, citing increased costs and a reduced level of care for the patient. Hospital administrators envisioned a massive and unmanageable influx of elderly patients to their facilities. Insurance companies feared they would be driven out of business by a government health plan that paid for medical and hospital treatment. Many Republican senators and congressmen also opposed the measure. But after reaching compromises with such powerful lobbying groups as the AMA and the American Hospital Association, Johnson and the Democrats in Congress prevailed. On July 30, 1965, the president signed into law a comprehensive medical care bill, declaring:

> No longer will older Americans be denied the healing miracle of modern medicine. No longer will illness crush and destroy the savings that they have so carefully put away over a lifetime so that they might enjoy dignity in their later years. No longer will young families see their own incomes, and their own hopes, eaten away simply because they are carrying out their deep moral obligations to their parents, and to their uncles, and their aunts.[83]

Medicare and Medicaid

The health care program established by Johnson's bill was not a part of the Economic Opportunity Act but rather was embodied in two amendments to the Social Security Act (Social Security, which provides economic assistance to retired and dis-

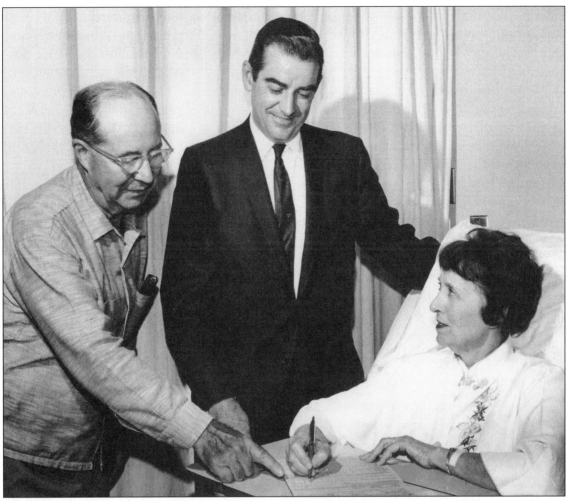

America's first Medicare beneficiary completes forms at an Illinois hospital in 1966. Medicare provided supplementary insurance for patients older than sixty-five.

abled people, was instituted by President Franklin Roosevelt in 1935). The first amendment, Medicare, gave hospital and supplementary medical insurance to Americans who were over the age of sixty-five and eligible for Social Security benefits. The costs of limited hospital stays and aftercare were covered, as were doctor bills and the expenses of home health care and outpatient hospital services. Funding for Medicare came from taxes and from premiums paid by the recipient of the services. The second amendment, called Medicaid, provided medical care for the needy, including those with low incomes regardless of age, the disabled, the blind, and families with dependent children. Following federal guidelines, the individual states would set up programs to provide care for the "medically needy" and would receive matching funds from the federal government.

From the outset the Medicare and Medicaid programs were extremely popular. For the first time the disadvantaged could afford the medical care that, in countless cases, they desperately needed. The programs turned out to be much more expensive than expected, however, and ways had to be found to cut costs. And critics still derided them as socialized medicine, destined to lead to higher costs and inferior health care. But doctors, who at first were opposed to Medicare, benefited by receiving increased income from Medicare payments, as did hospitals and other service providers. But the major beneficiaries of the new law were the elderly. Benefits from Medicare brought many senior citizens out of poverty. In 1966 the poverty rate for the elderly was 28.5 percent; two years later, that rate had declined to around 25 percent.

In his memoirs, Johnson recalled his Great Society's achievements in health care for the elderly. "I take pride and comfort," he wrote, "in the thought that . . . our senior citizens are enjoying medical care that would otherwise not have been available to them."[84]

The Poor and the Law

Although not one of the highly publicized programs such as Head Start or the community action agencies, Legal Services was nevertheless an important part of the War on Poverty, for it gave, and still gives, a legal voice to poor Americans. Stephen J. Pollack, who was assistant general counsel of the Office of Economic Opportunity explains why in the book, Launching the War on Poverty: An Oral History.

There are many Legal Services programs around the country. They have gotten into so many different areas where the poor never had lawyers. Throughout so much of the legal system, particularly on the civil side—and Legal Services is primarily on the civil side—persons of property and wealth had lawyers and used the legal system to preserve, protect, and improve their interests. The poor by and large did not have access to lawyers. Where they had good arguments, they weren't able to present them. Where they needed laws to protect them, our system requires lawyers to move the legislation along, and the poor didn't have lawyers. So this Legal Services Program changed the equation very greatly, and it still is.

Legal Services Program

The law was another area in which the Great Society sought to eradicate the causes of poverty. Lawyers have long felt a responsibility to help the less fortunate obtain legal services. Legal aid societies, sponsored by bar associations, have been in existence since the 1800s. By the 1960s there were hundreds of independent legal aid offices around the country, but they were staffed by underpaid and overworked attorneys. There had to be a better way to provide legal services to the poor. Supreme Court justice Arthur Goldberg had suggested to President Johnson that legal services be a part of the War on Poverty. At that time, Johnson said no. But Sargent Shriver felt differently, as Stephen J. Pollack, assistant general counsel of the OEO recalls:

> One thing that history ought to record is that in the very beginning, when we were starting to develop these ideas about the Legal Services Program, Shriver . . . said to me that he thought that the launching of the Legal Services Program would possibly be the most important thing that he would do in the poverty program. He said he felt this way because making provision for attorneys to represent the poor and for the courts to recognize the rights of the poor never before recognized would have such a far-reaching and continuing effect on the distribution of power in the society. I thought that was farsighted of him, and I shared his view. [85]

In 1965 the Legal Services Program was established by the Office of Economic Opportunity to give low-income people free access, through a national network of law firms, to the same legal services that middle-class citizens could afford. The first year's funding, through the Community Action Program, was six hundred thousand dollars. E. Clinton Bamberger, the first director of the Legal Services Program describes its mission:

> Our responsibility is to marshal the forces of law and the strength of lawyers to combat the causes and effects of poverty. Lawyers must uncover the legal causes of poverty, remodel the system which generates the cycle of poverty and design new social, legal, and political tools and vehicles to move people from deprivation, depression, and despair to opportunity, hope and ambition. [86]

The program provided legal services to the poor by representing them in court cases involving housing, health care, conflicts with utility companies, domestic violence, and employment problems. In 1967 an amendment to the Economic Opportunity Act prohibited Legal Services lawyers from handling criminal cases. As had happened with the neighborhood health centers, some opposition to the Legal Service centers arose. The American Bar Association (ABA), a professional group representing the nation's lawyers, saw the program as an example of the federal government meddling in the private practice of law. The association was already spending $5 million a year providing legal services to the poor. A compromise was ultimately reached giving the ABA the right to oversee the ethical practices of Legal Services lawyers, and the organization gave its support to the program.

Throughout its history, the Legal Services Program has been a controversial agency. It was the first time the federal government became directly involved in providing legal aid to the poor. Its detractors charged that Legal Services attorneys filed unnecessary but high-profile lawsuits to advance their own political interests. Despite these objections, the Legal Services Program gave thousands of poor people access to legal help they could never have afforded on their own. Donald Baker, general counsel to the OEO, sums up his opinion of the impact the Legal Services Program had:

I think in the long run that the impact of legal aid on the improvement of the lives of the poor . . . may be the most important thing that we are doing. Legal aid will have more impact on [the] total structure of our social, economic, and political structures than anything else that the OEO and perhaps even the federal government has done on the domestic scene in our lifetime. [87]

As the Great Society moved forward in the areas of jobs, education, the law, health, and community action, another movement was beginning to exert its influence on American society. The civil rights movement of the 1960s was established to work toward guaranteeing African Americans the full partnership in American life that they had so far been denied. No one could predict the violence that the movement would ignite nor the effect it would have on the War on Poverty.

Civil Rights and the Great Society

On May 17, 1954, the U.S. Supreme Court handed down a landmark decision that would forever change the legal status of African Americans in the United States. In the case of *Brown v. Board of Education of Topeka, Kansas,* the Court ruled that segregation in public schools was unconstitutional. This decision overturned more than half a century of legal separation between the races, fostered by an 1896 Supreme Court decision legalizing "separate but equal" facilities for blacks. From lunch counters and schools to public restrooms and even drinking fountains, segregation was permitted. In the South, states that were once part of the Confederacy passed laws to further curtail the rights of African Americans.

Legally, that changed with the *Brown* decision, which states that separate schools for blacks are, by their very nature, not equal to white schools. Practically, however, integration of U.S. schools would become a long and bitter struggle as African Americans marched, prayed, fought, and often died, to secure their rights. The civil rights movement of the sixties was a turbulent period in American history. It would have a significant impact on Lyndon Johnson's Great Society and the War on Poverty. When Johnson became president during that decade, his vision for eradicating poverty and building a Great Society included people of all races. He was keenly aware that African Americans had long been denied full participation in American life. While securing civil rights for all Americans was not officially a part of his Great Society, the advances he brought about through civil rights legislation made it a large part, and a great legacy, of Lyndon Johnson's administration.

Confronting Racism

After the landmark *Brown* decision, the struggle for civil rights gained momentum. Soon after Kennedy's inauguration in January 1961 several black college students in North Carolina staged a "sit-in" for being refused service at a local lunch counter. Before long, similar demonstrations were spreading across the South. In 1962 the University of Mississippi was ordered to admit James Meredith, its first black student. Kennedy faced a volatile situation when the segregationist governor of Mississippi, Ross Barnett, blocked Meredith from entering the university. Despite Kennedy's televised appeal for calm, and the presence of more than three hundred federal marshals, Meredith's entry into "Ole Miss" caused a riot that left two dead and hundreds injured. The next year saw an increase in violence, including the murder of Medgar Evers, a young, black civil rights worker who was brutally gunned down in front of his family. During this time of racial unrest, Kennedy was moving cautiously in considering civil rights legislation.

JFK's Civil Rights Bill

Some progress in civil rights had been made in Kennedy's first two years in office, as desegregation efforts began to open schools and public facilities to African Americans. But Kennedy was slow to advocate comprehensive civil rights legislation. He told Martin Luther King Jr. of the difficulties of trying to push a sweeping civil rights bill through Congress: "If we go into a long fight in Congress it will bottleneck everything else and still get no bill."[88] What he wanted was legislation that would not cause southern senators and congressmen to

In 1962 James Meredith became the first black student to enroll at the University of Mississippi.

President John F. Kennedy meets with civil rights leaders (Dr. Martin Luther King Jr. is on the left). After Kennedy was assassinated, President Johnson continued the fight for civil rights.

retaliate by opposing other legislation, such as a tax cut that Kennedy wanted.

But Democratic Senate leaders were pushing for action on civil rights, so Kennedy went on television on the evening of June 11, 1963, to tell the American public his plan for civil rights legislation.

I am . . . asking the Congress to enact legislation giving all Americans the right to be served in facilities which are open to the public—hotels, restaurants, theaters, retail stores and similar establishments. . . . I am also asking Congress to authorize the Federal government to participate more fully in lawsuits designed to end segregation in public education. . . . Other features will also be requested, including greater protection for the right to vote.[89]

Passing the Torch

While Congress was debating Kennedy's civil rights bill, racial violence continued. Then on November 22, 1963, President Kennedy was struck down by an assassin's bullets while on a campaign visit to Dallas, Texas. The quest for civil rights legislation now fell to the new president, Lyndon Johnson.

On November 27, 1963, five days after Kennedy's death, Johnson addressed

Congress in what was the first major speech of his presidency. In his address, the new president vowed to continue Kennedy's policies both at home and abroad:

> The greatest leader of our time has been struck down by the foulest deed of our time. Today John Fitzgerald Kennedy lives on in the immortal words and works that he left behind. . . . And now the ideas and ideals which he so nobly represented must and will be translated into effective action. . . . He said, "let us begin." Today, in this moment of new resolve, I would say to all my fellow Americans, "let us continue."[90]

There were many good reasons for Johnson to continue Kennedy's domestic programs. First was the desire to honor the fallen president by fulfilling his dreams for the nation. In doing so, Johnson would reassure Americans that the United States was strong enough to withstand the ultimate act of violence committed against its leader. Johnson also hoped to mobilize the vast resources of the federal government to help less fortunate Americans. Johnson thought back to his days as the head of the Texas National Youth Administration, and how Franklin Roosevelt's programs attacked the problems brought on by the Great Depression. In a conversation with Walter Heller, economic adviser to both Kennedy and Johnson, about his admiration for FDR's handling of the depression he said, "If you look at my record, you would know

that I am a Roosevelt New Dealer."[91] But Johnson the New Dealer was also Johnson the politician, and he knew full well that there was a presidential election coming up in 1964. He would take Kennedy's programs, including the civil rights bill, and by successfully implementing them, gain the public support necessary to win the presidency in his own right in 1964.

Still, no one really knew how committed Johnson, a Texas Democrat, would actually be to getting civil rights legislation through Congress. As a congressman and senator, he had voted against six previous civil rights bills. But over the years his attitudes had changed. Johnson knew "that segregation not only separated blacks and whites in the South but also separated the South from the rest of the nation. . . . An end to southern segregation would mean the full integration of the South into the Union, bringing with it economic progress and political influence comparable to that of other regions."[92] As Senate majority leader, Johnson supported the passage of civil rights bills in 1957 and 1960. By the time he became president, Johnson's resolve was clear: "When I sat in the Oval Office after President Kennedy died and reflected on civil rights, there was no question in my mind as to what I would do. I knew that, as President and as a man, I would use every ounce of strength I possessed to gain justice for the black American."[93] In Congress, however, many obstacles still loomed in the path of civil rights legislation.

The civil rights bill passed the House of Representatives on February 10, 1964. But its biggest battle lay ahead in the Senate, where southern Democrats, most of whom supported segregation, would try to defeat it. The means they would use was a filibuster: a series of continuous speeches, roll calls, and irrelevant motions on the Senate floor designed to impede and ultimately block proposed legislation. For three months the filibuster dragged on until enough opposition votes were finally secured to end the delay. Finally on June 10, 1964, the filibuster was ended. The Senate passed the bill on June 19 and on July 2 President Johnson signed the Civil Rights Act of 1964 into law.

Laying It on the Line

Equal opportunities for all citizens, regardless of color, was a priority for Lyndon Johnson's Great Society. How could America truly be great if a large segment of the population remained under the shadow of racial discrimination? The following excerpt is taken from Johnson's memoir, The Vantage Point.

The civil rights bill—designed to end segregation in public restaurants and hotels—was another matter. As an emotional issue, it contained the seeds of rebellion on Capitol Hill—not just over civil rights, but over my entire legislative program. As a moral issue, however, it could not be avoided regardless of the outcome. . . . I [pushed for civil rights legislation] . . . against the advice of staff members and long-time advisers whose judgment I greatly respected. I remember two particularly heated debates in the first few days of my presidency: one at my home, The Elms, and another in my office in the Executive Office Building. Some of those present urged me not to push for the civil rights bill. They did not think the bill could be passed.

"Mr. President," one of them said, "you should not lay the prestige of the Presidency on the line."

"What's it for if it's not to be laid on the line?" I asked. . . .

The issue could not be avoided. I was not just the President of Southern Americans or white Americans. I was the President of all Americans. I believed that a huge injustice had been perpetrated for hundreds of years on every black man, woman, and child in the United States. I did not think that our nation could endure much longer as a viable democracy if that injustice were allowed to continue.

Law and Backlash

The Civil Rights Act of 1964 banned racial discrimination in restaurants, hotels, parks, libraries, and other public places; encouraged the integration of public schools (which had already been mandated by a Supreme Court decision in 1954); and withheld federal funds from places that practiced discrimination. It also established the Equal Employment Opportunity Commission to bring cases of employment discrimination to the courts. African Americans now had legal backing to their struggle to attain civil rights. But the demonstrations and urban unrest that accompanied that struggle was beginning to take a toll on those who were not a part of the movement. Alabama governor George Wallace became a candidate for president in the 1964 elections, campaigning on a platform of opposition to civil rights. And many whites were listening to his message. According to Johnson, Wallace's strong following "brought the term 'white backlash' into our vocabulary, a shorthand phrase for growing white resentment against the pace and tone of Negro demands."[94] This backlash against growing violence began to diminish white sympathy for the civil rights movement, especially as the movement gradually migrated north.

In 1964 many large northern industrial cities such as Chicago and New York began experiencing racial disturbances. In the summer of 1965 in Watts, a mostly black section of Los Angeles, three days of rioting resulted in thirty-four people dead, thousands injured, and property damage of more than $40 million. That same summer President Johnson signed into law another landmark civil rights law. The Voting Rights Act of 1965 banned literacy tests for voters. In many southern states prospective voters had to pass a test to be eligible to cast their ballot. White and black voters were given different tests. Tests given to blacks were usually so difficult that passing them was impossible. One test, for example, required blacks to recite the entire U.S. Constitution. The act also authorized the use of federal examiners to assist in the registering of black voters in several southern states. By the end of the year, some 250,000 new black voters had been registered.

Over the next three years many U.S. cities, mostly in the North, experienced some 150 riots. This escalating violence signaled a rift in the civil rights movement, as younger blacks became impatient with the nonviolence advocated by such traditional movement leaders as Martin Luther King. "Black Power" became the rallying cry of the new militant wing of the civil rights movement. For middle-class whites, growing black militancy was a new and disturbing aspect of the civil rights movement. And it began having an effect on the War on Poverty. According to authors Maurice Isserman and Michael Kazin, "White working-class taxpayers, and property owners, already fearful about blacks moving into their neighborhoods, resented the war on poverty as a payoff to rioters."[95] In their minds, spending money for law and order became more important

Three stores burn during the 1965 Los Angeles race riots. The three-day riot in the city's Watts neighborhood left thirty-four people dead and thousands injured.

than funding poverty programs. When Johnson announced a new jobs program after riots in 1967, the program, which served mostly poor African Americans, was seen by critics as a program established to reward black rioters.

Many middle-class whites fled the cities and purchased homes in the suburbs, which were financially out of reach of poor inner-city blacks. Bumper stickers proclaiming such sentiments as "I Fight Poverty, I Work" displayed the middle class's growing disenchantment with Johnson's poverty program. They felt that

they were losing their own freedoms and began resenting the fact that a part of their hard-earned income was going for taxes to support poverty programs. One Chicago resident complained, "We work hard, pay our taxes, improve ourselves, only to find the more we improve ourselves and our property the more we are taxed and told what we can and cannot do with it."[96]

Civil Rights and Poverty

In the inner cities, poverty had become a festering sore among the black population, and with it, violence seemed inevitable. It

The Poor People's Campaign

In April 1968, less than a month after Martin Luther King Jr. was assassinated, a group of African Americans, poor whites, Hispanics, and Native Americans began a march to Washington, D.C. It was the beginning of the Poor People's Campaign, which was designed to shed light on the plight of the poor of all races and colors. William Rutherford, head of the civil rights organization the Southern Christian Leadership Conference, describes the march in the book Voices of Freedom: An Oral History of the Civil Rights Movement from the 1950s Through the 1980s.

[The purpose of the Poor People's Campaign] was to gather the poorest of the poor in the nation's capital, the heart of the wealthiest country in the world, to camp them, these homeless, hungry people, in the heart of this city and its fabulous malls situated between the Lincoln Memorial and the Washington Monument, take the plea and the complaint of the poor to each of the government agencies. To take them to the Department of Agriculture, where they deal with food. To take them to the Department of Justice, where they deal with laws and the application of laws. To take them to the Department of the Interior, where the Chicanos and the Native Americans have very serious problems of land tenure and so on. The thrust, the tactic of the Poor People's Campaign was in dealing with our own government to focus and attract the attention of the world on these problems, which are everpresent, but which by and large are largely ignored by the masses of Americans or which are not really focused on by the masses of Americans.

Senators and civil rights leaders meet during the Poor People's Campaign.

was not just the violence of the street riots, but a more personal, more painful kind. As a young black man in Harlem explains:

So, all these frustrations build up in the black man day after day. The system that we live in becomes a vicious cycle and there is never a way out. He begs for a change and it seems that the conditions get worse and worse and never make a move towards the better. And we find that for every step forward, we are forced by the powers that be to take five steps backward into even more deplorable conditions. So, when this anger builds up in black people, not knowing how to let it out and how to retaliate against the power structures, the black man finds a way out; but the way out is often in the bottle of wine or a needle containing heroin or in a reefer, or in the power of his fists when he slaps his wife down. The woman finds a way out in the power of her hand when she slaps a child down, and so the cycle goes on.[97]

As that cycle was making the sixties into one of the most turbulent decades in U.S. history, civil rights for blacks became increasingly identified, in the minds of the American public, as the social priority of the Great Society. Virtually ignored as the symbol of the War on Poverty was the plight of poor white coal miners in Appalachia, their place taken by the black poor of the inner cities. Historian John Andrew observes that "the War on Poverty rested as much on civil rights as it did on economics. And when civil rights idealism turned to racial divisiveness, the backlash spilled over to the antipoverty effort, producing a crisis for liberals that was highlighted by the Watts riots."[98]

The crisis brought on by the white-middle-class reaction to Johnson's civil rights policy was not the only blow to be struck against the War on Poverty. It was about to be overshadowed by another, more dangerous international crisis. For while Johnson was fighting the War on Poverty at home, half a world away another war was being fought by young American soldiers, who confronted an elusive enemy in the jungles and rice paddies of a place called Vietnam.

Guns or Butter?

When Lyndon Johnson became president in 1963, he inherited U.S. interest in a struggle for control of Vietnam, a nation in Southeast Asia. Vietnam was divided roughly in half, with a Communist regime ruling North Vietnam and a non-communist government in power in South Vietnam. Beginning in the late 1940s, U.S. foreign policy toward communism was one of "containment," that is, limiting the spread of the Communist ideology around the world. As Communist guerrillas from North Vietnam began infiltrating the south in an effort to overthrow the government there, the United States sent military equipment and advisers to South Vietnam. By the time of Kennedy's assassination, there were sixteen thousand U.S. military advisers in Vietnam.

A few days after Johnson became president he pledged that the U.S. government would provide "full unity of support for established U.S. policy in South Vietnam."[99] He hoped to resolve the conflict quickly so he could turn his full attention to his Great Society programs. He was also anxious about a wider war that could take money away from his antipoverty efforts. Johnson continued to send U.S. aid to South Vietnam in the form of advisers, equipment, and money, hoping that South Vietnam could eventually defeat the Communist threat from North Vietnam.

Escalating the War

In the fall of 1964, while Johnson campaigned for his election as president that November, Communist guerrilla fighters known as Vietcong continued their attacks against the U.S. and South Vietnamese military. One Vietcong raid, in February 1965, (shortly after Johnson's inauguration) killed eight U.S. soldiers. Johnson ordered a series of retaliatory air strikes on military installations in North Vietnam. These strikes were followed by a sustained program of bombing raids on North Vietnam called Operation Rolling Thunder. On March 8 the first U.S. combat troops, marines of the Ninth Marine Expeditionary Brigade, went ashore at Danang, South Vietnam. These marines were just the beginning of Johnson's massive military buildup in Vietnam: at the height of the war more than half a million Americans would be fighting in Southeast Asia.

Back home, Lyndon Johnson's other war, the War on Poverty, would soon begin to feel the effects of the war in Vietnam.

Guns and Butter

Johnson did not order America's escalation of the Vietnam conflict without being concerned about the damaging effect it would have on his domestic programs. It

Johnson and the War

As the Vietnam War escalated, Lyndon Johnson found himself in a virtually impossible position. While the war kept taking more and more of America's resources, Johnson clung to the vain hope that he could keep his poverty programs financially afloat. In his book Lyndon Johnson's War: America's Cold War Crusade in Vietnam, *Michael H. Hunt describes Johnson's dilemma.*

In the face of adversity on the battlefield and at home, Johnson stuck to what he regarded as a moderate policy. He would not give in to the demands of the Joint Chiefs of Staff and other hawks to expand the ground war beyond the borders of South Vietnam or lift restrictions on bombing. He would not play appeaser, a role sure to create havoc in Southeast Asia and perhaps beyond and set in question the American reputation as a determined, reliable superpower and global force for good. Nor would he allow Vietnam to destroy his legislative achievements, arguing that the country could have war and prosperity and Great Society programs all at the same time. Johnson later recalled his rationale: "After all, our country was built by pioneers who had a rifle in one hand and an ax in the other to build their homes and provide for their families."

had happened before: in the aftermath of the Spanish-American War, the First and Second World Wars, even Korea, the progress of American social programs had slowed. Johnson later reflected on the dilemma he found himself in during early 1965:

> I knew from the start that I was bound to be crucified either way I moved. If I left the woman I really loved—the Great Society—in order to get involved with that . . . war on the other side of the world, then I would lose everything at home. All my programs. All my hopes to feed the hungry and shelter the homeless. All my dreams to provide education and medical care to the browns and the blacks and the lame and the poor. But if I left that war and let the Communists take over South Vietnam, then I would be seen as a coward and my nation would be seen as an appeaser and we would both find it impossible to accomplish anything for anybody anywhere on the entire globe.[100]

Despite this later recollection, at the time Johnson appeared to believe otherwise. "I believe we can do both," he said. "We are the nation with the highest GNP [gross national product], the highest wages, and the most people at work. We can do both. And as long as I am president we will do both."[101] With this attitude guiding him, Johnson set the course for America's war in Vietnam. Bombing raids and troop deployments steadily increased. By the end of 1965 there were almost two hundred thousand U.S. troops in Vietnam, and more were on the way. Soon it had become increasingly clear that the war would not be over quickly. As 1966 approached, Johnson knew he had to talk to the American people about Vietnam and the Great Society in his State of the Union address.

Most economists agree that a nation cannot afford both guns (that is, military expenditures) and butter (domestic programs). In his State of the Union speech, Johnson was determined to convince the American people of his conviction that he could provide both guns and butter. The creation of the speech began with several members of Johnson's administration trying to put together a draft acceptable to the president. When this led to less than satisfactory results, they called on former speechwriter Richard Goodwin for help. Goodwin had left the administration a few months earlier but agreed to work on the new speech. Countless drafts were submitted to Johnson, who sent them back for revisions. With the January 12 deadline approaching, Goodwin labored for thirty-six hours straight and finally, on the morning of the twelfth, delivered to Johnson what he called the "guns and butter" speech. After additional changes were made the speech was ready, and at 9:00 P.M. Johnson stepped before a joint session of Congress to ask the senators and congressmen to approve a new round of Great Society programs, while at the same time fund the war in

In his 1966 State of the Union address, President Johnson declared that the government could afford both military expenditures and social programs.

Vietnam. Johnson declared that "we will not permit those who fire upon us in Vietnam to win a victory over the desires and intentions of all the American people. This Nation is mighty enough, its society is healthy enough, its people are strong enough, to pursue our goals in the rest of the world while still building a Great Society here at home."[102]

Johnson went on to appeal for continued funding for the War on Poverty, and listed new Great Society programs he envisioned, including rebuilding big city slums, increasing support for law enforcement, cleaning up America's rivers, and ending housing discrimination. Johnson said America's economy was strong enough to pay for these programs and would even show a cash surplus by 1967. But many in Congress were skeptical of Johnson's optimistic economic outlook. Congressman Bill Barrett pointedly asked, "Where are we going to get the money?"[103] It was the essential question that Johnson had managed to ignore.

A Recalcitrant Congress

It takes money to fight any war, whether the enemy is a foreign aggressor or a domestic problem such as poverty. As America's involvement in Vietnam escalated throughout 1966 and 1967, so did the cost of waging the war. Despite Johnson's early confidence that the United States could afford both wars, reality was proving him wrong. The war and changes in Congress were making it difficult for Johnson to get new legislation passed. According to the *Congressional Quarterly:*

> Mr. Johnson's success in 1967 did not nearly meet his historic accomplishments in getting landmark Great Society legislation through the overwhelmingly

Democratic 89th Congress (1965–1966). The specter of the war in Viet Nam coupled with the shift to the GOP [Republican Party] of 47 House seats and three Senate seats in the 1966 election gave the President a relatively hostile Congress which was intent on holding down Government spending.

Accordingly, the President introduced little in the way of new Great Society programs, preferring instead to improve and expand already enacted programs. . . . Even some of these proposals . . . faced serious trouble. [104]

Vietnam was consuming a greater and greater portion of the American economy, and that forced Johnson to consider asking for a tax increase—something he had long been trying to avoid. It also spelled the beginning of the end of his dreams for a Great Society.

President Johnson meets with troops in Vietnam. Johnson's domestic programs suffered as a result of the money spent to finance America's involvement in Vietnam.

Wilbur Mills was a powerful congressman and chairman of the House Ways and Means Committee, the body that handles all legislation concerning taxes and public financing. Although Mills was a Democrat, he remained unconvinced that Johnson's tax increase was necessary, or that it would even make it through Congress. In exchange for his support of the new tax, Mills gave Johnson some conditions. He told the president, "You have to go on TV [and say that] because of Vietnam we must cut domestic spending and pass a tax increase. I also want some commitments made . . . on major slashes in domestic spending." [105]

For the first time in his long political career, Lyndon Johnson, usually a master of negotiation had no choice but to accept a major compromise. "The skillful trader," wrote Doris Kearns, "his bargaining position enfeebled, now had to give up what he wanted to get what he needed." [106]

Herbert Kramer, the OEO's director of public affairs, recalls the shock of budget cuts:

[It was when the] budget was returned by the Budget Bureau that the first shock of the impact of Vietnam seeped in. It didn't seep in; it hit with a hammer blow! . . . Mr. Shriver did his best to put a good cloak on that and make it seem that these expenditures were adequate. He was at all times a loyal subject of Mr. Johnson, but there was no cloaking the fact that the program had to be drastically curtailed and cut back, and the expression "the War on Poverty" soon became a rather hollow mockery. [107]

With a rising budget deficit, Johnson knew that the tax increase was the only way to keep his commitment in Vietnam alive and still hope that his Great Society programs would somehow continue. The American public, however, was opposed to a tax increase and wanted instead to see a reduction in federal spending to help the economy. Those who were against the Vietnam War also opposed the tax increase, hoping that as more of Johnson's poverty programs suffered from lack of funding, the more inclined he might be to keep them going by reducing spending on Vietnam. Republicans said that what America needed was not more social programs but some assurance that the ones already put in place by the Great Society were working.

Johnson's tax bill became a source of lengthy debate in Congress. Conservatives wanted the money to go to fight the war in Vietnam, while liberals insisted that all funds generated by the tax increase should go for domestic programs only. To Johnson's dismay, the bill would remain stalled in Senator Mills's Ways and Means Committee for eighteen months.

Thus, with no tax increase in the foreseeable future, Johnson had no choice but to begin making cuts in Great Society programs. Although Johnson wanted an appropriation of around $2.06 billion for the Office of Economic Opportunity, the agency received only $1.77 billion. Meanwhile, the war in Vietnam was expanding. By the end of 1967 nearly sixteen thousand Americans had been killed and another one hundred thousand wounded. Despite lifting certain restrictions on the bombing of North Vietnam, the United States was no closer to winning the war. Americans began questioning Johnson's handling of the war, and the president's popular approval began to wane. Antiwar protests by college students spread throughout the country, and young men burned their draft cards to demonstrate their opposition to the war. America plunged deeper into the war that was often called a "quagmire."

Johnson Withdraws

The next year, 1968, began with a devastating attack on U.S. forces in Vietnam. On January 30, the first day of the Vietnamese New Year, called Tet, the Vietcong launched the largest offensive of the war. More than one hundred South Vietnamese cities became targets of Vietcong raids, including the capital city of Saigon, where the U.S. embassy was attacked. Although the Tet Offensive turned out to be a failure for the Communists, who suffered thousands of casualties, it stunned the United States into the realization that there was no safe haven for Americans anywhere in South Vietnam.

In the aftermath of the Tet Offensive, Johnson's public image took its worst beating. All along he had told the American people that the United States was winning the war; now it was obvious that victory was still far off, and the trust Americans had placed in his leadership was damaged beyond repair. "By 1968," wrote Doris Kearns, "Johnson had lost this trust. The issue was not simply Johnson's loss of popularity; it was his loss of credibility. A majority of people believed he regularly lied to them." [108] His overall approval rating plummeted from 48 percent to 36 percent, and only one out of four Americans agreed with his handling of the war. In addition, 1968 was an election year, and in the New Hampshire primary election, Democratic senator Eugene McCarthy, a peace candidate whose message appealed to opponents of the Vietnam War, made a strong showing. It was another indication that perhaps Lyndon Johnson's time had passed.

For some time Johnson had considered not running for another term as president. He had discussed it with his family and with several close aides, but had never made a firm decision. With the events of early 1968 still swirling around him, however, Johnson finally made up his mind. On March 31, 1968, Johnson addressed the nation via television from the Oval Office. He announced that he was ordering a halt to most of the bombing of North Vietnam. Then, he somberly declared that he would neither seek nor accept the Democratic nomination for another term as president.

Seven months later Americans elected a new president. Amid war, demonstrations, and political strife, Lyndon Johnson handed the presidency and its problems to Republican Richard M. Nixon. He left behind a nation divided over a seemingly endless war in Asia and civil strife at home, a nation that had lost trust in Johnson as their leader. His dreams of a Great Society and victory in the War on Poverty were stalled by the expense of Vietnam. Opponents blasted

Johnson's Farewell

On March 31, 1968, Lyndon Johnson gave the most difficult speech of his presidency. Knowing that he had lost the confidence of the American people, that the war in Vietnam was draining the money from his beloved Great Society, and that the nation was deeply divided over the war, Johnson faced the television cameras that had been set up in the Oval Office. The dark circles under his eyes and the lines etched on his face by years of struggling to balance two wars clearly showed as he spoke. The following excerpt from Johnson's speech is taken from the Lyndon Baines Johnson Library and Museum website.

Tonight I want to speak to you of peace in Vietnam and Southeast Asia. . . . I have ordered our aircraft and our naval vessels to make no attacks on North Vietnam, except in the area north of the demilitarized zone where the continuing enemy buildup directly threatens allied forward positions and where movements of their troops and supplies are clearly related to that threat. . . . Our purpose in this action is to bring about a reduction in the level of violence that now exists. It is to save the lives of brave men— and to save the lives of innocent women and children. It is to permit the contending forces to move closer to a political settlement. . . .

With America's sons in the fields far away, with America's future under challenge right there at home, with our hopes and the world's hopes for peace in the balance every day, I do not believe that I should devote an hour or a day of my time to any personal partisan causes or to any duties other than the awesome duties of this office—the Presidency of your country.

Accordingly, I shall not seek, and I will not accept, the nomination of my party for another term as your president.

President Johnson announces that he plans to refuse the 1968 Democratic presidential nomination.

his programs as wasteful and ineffective failures. For example, critics seized on the fact that many Job Corps facilities were operating at less than their full capacity. Also, in numerous community action agencies, federal funding was wasted on bureaucratic incompetence and neighborhood projects that limped along unproductively, only to disappear when the government money ran out. The War on Poverty was an unfinished war of a different kind, but no less painful to Johnson. In his memoirs, Johnson lamented:

> I tried to make it possible for every child of every color to grow up in a nice house, eat a solid breakfast, to attend a decent school and to get a good and lasting job. I asked so little in return, just a little thanks. Just a little appreciation. That's all. But look what I got instead. Riots in 175 cities. Looting. Burning. Shooting. . . . Young people by the thousands leaving the university, marching in the streets, chanting that horrible song about how many kids I had killed that day. . . . It ruined everything.[109]

Johnson's poverty programs were now in the hands of a new president, but his legacy rested with future generations who, he hoped, would benefit from his War on Poverty and the Great Society. "If the American people don't love me," he said, "their descendants will."[110]

Chapter

9

The Legacy of the Great Society

Even before he became president, Richard Nixon was skeptical about the prospects for success of Johnson's Great Society programs, including the War on Poverty. Nixon wrote in his memoirs, "I could see that Johnson had fallen into the trap that snares so many believers in big government: he was promising far more than ever could be achieved. . . . The Great Society promised so much to so many that, instead of inspiring people to work hard to attain its goals, it made people impatient and angry when the goals were not immediately achieved without effort on their part. "[111] After his election, Nixon wanted to "get rid of the costly failures of the Great Society—and . . . do it immediately." [112]

Beginning of the End

Nixon had always disliked the Office of Economic Opportunity, seeing it as a manifestation of the "big government" endorsed by the Democratic Party. In contrast, Nixon felt that power should be vested in the individual states, where governors, mayors, and city councils made the decisions on behalf of their constituents. The Republicans called this decentralization of power the "New Federalism." It differed from the War on Poverty's programs in that Johnson's programs bypassed elected state and local officials. Under Johnson, the federal government set goals for the nation and expected those goals to be carried out at the local level. The New Federalism sought to return power to those officials.

On August 8, 1969, Nixon gave a televised speech about his proposed reforms of domestic programs under the banner of New Federalism. "For a third of a century," Nixon said, "power and responsibility have flowed toward Washington. . . . We intend to reverse this tide, and to turn back to the States a greater measure of responsibility—not as a way of avoiding problems, but as a better way of solving problems."[113] The president did not abolish the OEO immediately, but instead began to reduce its influence and power. Under Donald Rumsfeld, Nixon's first director of the OEO, the agency lost its administrative responsibilities over key poverty programs. The plan was to turn the Office of Economic Opportunity into a "laboratory agency" where new social programs could be developed and, if found workable, would be transferred to other government agencies for implementation.

In 1971 Nixon made several proposals for revenue sharing, in which federal funds would be distributed to states and municipalities to use, with only broad guidelines from the federal government as to how the money could be spent. Covered by a special revenue sharing program were the War on Poverty's community action agencies. Nixon felt that the local agencies had not been successful enough to warrant specific federal funding, declaring that, "Little justification for continuing separate categorical funding can be identified. Evidence is lacking that community action agencies are moving substantial numbers of people out of poverty on a self-sustaining basis."[114]

After taking office in 1969, President Richard Nixon vowed to do away with Johnson's Great Society programs.

Under revenue sharing, municipalities could use funds for community action agencies, or they could choose to spend the money in other ways if they so desired. What this meant for the Office of Economic Opportunity, as Nixon well knew, was that it would no longer be necessary and could be dismantled.

In early 1973 Nixon submitted a budget to Congress that included no funding for the Office of Economic Opportunity. Weakened by the lack of money and the transfer of various programs to other federal agencies, the OEO barely continued to survive. Nixon might have eliminated it altogether if he had not been embroiled in what became known as the Watergate scandal, which forced him to resign the presidency in July 1974. His successor, Gerald Ford, oversaw the creation of the Community Services Administration, an agency responsible for funding and management of the community action agencies. With the implementation of this new federal agency, the OEO ceased to exist.

The Community Services Administration continued to operate until the administration of Ronald Reagan, who, in 1981, rescinded the Economic Opportunity Act, replacing it with the Community Services Block Grant program. This program continues to provide the community action agencies with funds to fight poverty at the local level. In 2001, nearly $600 million in block grants was available to community action agencies that cover more than 95 percent of all counties in the United States.

Government and the Needy

The Declaration of Independence proclaims that "all men are created equal, that they are endowed by their Creator with certain unalienable Rights, that among these are Life, Liberty and the pursuit of Happiness." This majestic document further states that governments are created to secure these rights for the people. But if all people are equal in the eyes of the Creator, certainly circumstances place different people in vastly unequal situations. A baby born in an urban ghetto may enter the world with the same rights as a baby born in an affluent suburb, but the ability of both to secure the fruits of these rights later in life will be markedly different. What responsibility, then, does the U.S. government have toward those in society who are less fortunate?

As far back as the colonial era, Americans recognized the plight of the poor. In 1642 the Plymouth Colony enacted the first poor law in America, providing relief for the poor, apprentice training for youth, and workhouses for those who were physically able. Poor people who were unable to work were sent to poorhouses, which sheltered and fed them at public expense. In the early twentieth century, Franklin D. Roosevelt's New Deal created scores of government programs to put the unemployed to work and help stabilize the U.S. economy. As a part of the New Deal, young Lyndon Johnson was able to observe its operation firsthand, and the experience had a direct effect on his own poverty programs. But the New Deal was created as a response to the nation's worst economic crisis: the Great Depression. During such a catastrophe, the government would be expected to do something to help those most affected, in the same way that regions hit by such natural disasters as floods and forest fires are designated federal disaster areas. In contrast, Johnson's Great Society was established during the sixties, a time of great economic prosperity. The very fact that this prosperity existed would give the president new avenues of funding for helping the poor.

For Johnson, poverty was "a call for action, a call for a revolutionary new program to attack one of the most stubbornly entrenched social ills in America."[115] And he took personally the responsibility of government helping the needy:

We foresaw clearly the problems and dangers. But the powerful conviction that an attack on poverty was right and necessary blotted out any fears that this program was a political landmine. Harry Truman used to say that 13 or 14 million Americans had their interests represented in Washington, but that the rest of the people had to depend on the President of the United States. That is how I felt about 35 million American poor. They had no voice and no champion. Whatever the cost, I was determined to represent them. Through me they would have an advocate and, I believed, new hope.[116]

But Johnson looked beyond the poor for beneficiaries of his programs. As he later wrote, "a program that eliminated poverty—or even reduced it—would strengthen the moral fiber of the entire country. It was on that basis that I prepared to move forward and commit the resources and prestige of the new administration."[117]

That Johnson saw himself, and by extension the government, as champion of the poor is evident in the vast number of programs initiated by the Great Society. As Joseph A. Califano, Johnson's assistant for domestic affairs from 1965 to 1969, recalls:

Johnson converted the federal government into a far more energetic, proactive force for social justice, striking down discriminatory practices and offering a hand up with education, health care, and job training. These functions had formerly been the preserve of private charities and the states. Before the Johnson administration, for example, the federal government was not training a single worker. He vested the federal government with the responsibility to soften the sharp elbows of capitalism and give it a beating, human heart; to redistribute opportunity as well as wealth.[118]

But it was that vast number of Great Society programs, and the speed at which they were launched, that led to the downfall of many of them. In the haste to get the Great Society under way, many of its programs were disorganized, wasteful with government funds, and even corrupt. The Community Action Program, for example, seemed especially susceptible to misguidance. Early in the program, a disproportionate amount of funding went to nationally based programs, leaving fewer dollars for local use. Many of the people running

Encouraging Dependency?

The Great Society promised a "hand up, not a handout." But some critics argue that such govern-ment involvement has, in fact, had the opposite effect. The following is taken from Sam Brown's "Self-Help: New Roots to an Old Idea" on the James MacGregor Burns Academy of Leadership website.

Ever since the New Deal began, the federal government has been creating social service pro-grams for poor people. . . . There are millions of people who are better off today because of Medicare, Head Start, and other social programs. But, bit by bit, the cumulative effect of all these programs has been to strip away from individuals the sure sense that they have control over their own lives.

Despite our best intentions, we have encouraged the poor to be dependent which in turn has made them objects of scorn for those who wish to help them. Instead of encouraging the poor to help themselves we have told them to wait for the federal grant or the expert solution that is sure to come. . . . We have, in short, created a system of helping that encourages the poor to be passive rather than active, dependent rather than self-reliant, recipients rather than producers, clients instead of people proud of their own work. We have divided the poor from the working, even though the poor are the most self-reliant people in America and have to be in order to survive. We have allowed those who wish to scorn the poor the opportunity to fos-ter the myth that poor people will not pull their own weight.

local organizations had little or no admin-istrative experience, leading to inefficient-ly run operations that wasted resources. In Chicago, for example, a federal grant fund-ed a job training program run by two rival street gangs. Still, to those living in abject poverty, it seemed that finally someone was taking an interest in helping them out of their seemingly hopeless condition.

Johnson built his Great Society on the concepts of community action and equal opportunity. Community action led to local involvement in the antipoverty process, a reminder of Johnson's teaching years. In stressing equal opportunity, the Great Society endeavored to give the poor a hand up, not a handout. Poor people would, through education and job training, remove the barriers that held them in poverty and allow them to build a better life for themselves and their families. Of course, the idea of helping people help themselves did not originate with the Great Society. But Johnson's strong commitment to the poor in a time of economic prosperity sets the Great Society apart from other presidents' programs that came before.

To be sure, some of Johnson's programs, such as Medicare, had their begin-

nings in past administrations. But one of Lyndon Johnson's greatest dreams was to equal, and even surpass, the social advances made by Franklin Roosevelt's New Deal. This he did by providing federal assistance to public schools through the Elementary and Secondary Education Act and the

Job Corps recruits attend class. Johnson designed the Job Corps and other programs to empower the poor through education and job training.

Higher Education Act. The arts and humanities were supported through federal endowments. And the Department of Transportation and Department of Housing and Urban Development were established to help improve the American quality of life. Although Johnson once called himself a "Roosevelt New Dealer," his legacy is firmly entrenched within the Great Society he created.

Perhaps the most important manifestation of Johnson's goal of equal opportunity can be found in his civil rights legislation. The landmark Civil Rights Act of 1964 and Voting Rights Act of 1965 gave blacks a new chance at equality in society and in the voting booth. Not since the end of the Civil War had such advances in African American equality been put forth. "We had come a long way," Johnson wrote in his memoirs. "In five short years we had put into law our promises of equality—at the ballot box, the employment center, the jury, the public inn, the public school, and the private housing market."[119]

Lyndon Johnson had seen his dream of a Great Society started only to see it crippled by the war in Vietnam. But for those looking back from the vantage point of later years, one question remained.

Who Won the War on Poverty?

In his State of the Union address delivered before Congress on January 25, 1988, President Ronald Reagan summed up his view of the War on Poverty that America had been fighting for more than two decades. "My friends, some years ago, the federal government declared war on poverty, and poverty won."[120] Did poverty in fact triumph over all attempts to conquer it? Was Johnson's War on Poverty in reality a failure? The answers to these questions depend on who is answering. Since 1964, numerous articles and books have analyzed the effectiveness of the War on Poverty. The authors of an essay entitled "Will the War on Poverty Change America?" describe the differing viewpoints on the War on Poverty:

> The war on poverty has been greeted by sharp criticism from friends as well as opponents, liberals as well as conservatives. It has been interpreted as a war *on* the poor. . . . Described as "a mockery," "a deliberate fraud" and "a conservative embracing of the status quo," it has also been characterized as a gimmick designed to show that poverty can be eliminated without changing the structure of society to reduce inequalities. . . .
>
> Its supporters defend it as an effort to begin to deal with the problems of the poor; as the best that could be carried through Congress, considering other pressing requirements (like that of keeping federal expenditures to less than $100 billion); as a set of programs that has some chance of success and is likely to improve and expand over the years. They are concerned with the pragmatics of political possibility.[121]

Politically conservative observers of the Great Society were quick to criticize the War

Johnson's Legacy

The following assessment of Lyndon Johnson's Great Society is from Elba K. Brown-Collier's article in Review of Social Economy *entitled "Johnson's Great Society: Its Legacy in the 1990s."*

When Johnson quickly pushed through his agenda for the "Great Society," it was clear no single policy or program was assumed to solve the problems of poverty in America. Many of the goals and objectives had little to do with specific programs. Johnson believed the details and implementation would be worked out later. It is also safe to assume that he did not believe only one method should or would be tried. What is the legacy of Johnson's "Great Society"? The historical data . . . [shows] that federal spending on programs identified with the "Great Society" increased after the legislative actions and remains higher as a percentage of the GDP [gross domestic product] and as a percentage of total federal outlay than before. Is the legacy the staying power of these programs? I would argue yes. . . . [Many studies show] that poverty would be much higher today were it not for the programs and policies we associate with the "War on Poverty," even though these have been reviewed and revised in light of our experience over the last 30 years.

Have we won the "War on Poverty"? Obviously not. Have we achieved the "Great Society" with all of its promises? No. But the legacy of Johnson and his vision is that we still ask why not!

on Poverty. One commentator remarked in 1984 that "from the first evaluation reports in the mid-sixties and continuing to the present day, the results of these [Great Society antipoverty] programs have been disappointing to their advocates and evidence of failure to their critics." [122]

Those critics charged that the War on Poverty was a misguided attempt to solve the problem of poverty by throwing money at it, creating a myriad of programs that were often disorganized, were sometimes used more for political activism than for helping the disadvantaged, and made the poor even more dependent on the federal government. "There is no question," said President Reagan, "that many well-intentioned Great Society–type programs contributed to family breakups, welfare dependency, and a large increase in births out of wedlock." [123]

Even those who were involved in the creation of the War on Poverty ultimately looked back to see the lost opportunities of the Great Society. "President Reagan said the war on poverty was a failure," says Sargent Shriver, the first director of the

Office of Economic Opportunity. "It was not a great success, that's true, because we didn't have the money. I told Lyndon Johnson myself that we needed two or three times the money we had to overcome the problem."[124] Robert A. Levine, assistant director of the OEO for planning and research, views the War on Poverty as a noble effort that could not fully succeed due to uncontrollable circumstances:

For a while, those of us charged with planning for the Office of Economic Opportunity really thought that we could abolish poverty in the United States; our plan showed us how. We were wrong, of course. One can blame the failure on politics, our own ineptitude and/or the Vietnam war. But politics always overrides "expertise" in running public programs—fortunately for democratic government. Ineptitude is the prudent assumption, and major outside events will always interfere.[125]

Despite its failures and critics, the War on Poverty has its defenders as well. "We did not end poverty," Levine says. "But we opened opportunities for a lot of people. We helped many to get out of poverty, and we induced change in vital public and private institutions."[126]

Among those voicing a strong belief in the value of the Great Society's poverty programs is Joseph Califano, who characterizes conservative assertions that the Great Society was a failure as "the political scam of the 20th century." The War on Poverty was, he says, "a focused, tenacious effort to revolutionize the role of the federal government with a series of interventions that enriched the lives of millions of Americans."[127]

Many Great Society programs are still providing help to the disadvantaged. Head Start has served more than 21 million children since its inception, enrolling more than 912,000 children in 2002 alone. The Job Corps helps more than 70,000 students at over 100 centers nationwide. It has given vocational, academic, and social training to more than 2 million young people since 1964. Medicaid and Medicare are still providing needed health care for millions of poor and elderly Americans.

With such differing viewpoints surrounding the outcome of the War on Poverty, can the success or failure of the Great Society really be determined? Perhaps statistics can provide an answer. In 1961 there were 45 federal social programs; by 1969 that number had increased to 435. At the beginning of the War on Poverty in 1964, 22.2 percent of Americans were living below the poverty line. In 1970 that number had dropped to 12.6 percent, the largest decrease in such a short period of time. In 2001 the poverty line stood at 11.7 percent, a slight increase over the previous year. This means that at the beginning of the twenty-first century, 32.9 million Americans still suffer the hardships of living in poverty. It is obvious that even for the richest nation on the earth, poverty is still a serious problem. But it might be even worse had it not been for the poverty programs of the Great Society.

Notes

Introduction: Lyndon Johnson's Great Society

1. Quoted in Robert Dallek, *Lone Star Rising: Lyndon Johnson and His Times, 1908–1960.* New York: Oxford University Press, 1991, p. 78.
2. Lyndon B. Johnson, *My Hope for America.* New York: Random House, 1964, p. 60.

Chapter 1: Poverty in the Sixties

3. Michael Harrington, *The Other America: Poverty in the United States.* New York: Macmillan, 1964, p. 1
4. Harrington, *The Other America,* pp. 1, 2.
5. Harrington, *The Other America,* p. 2.
6. John Kenneth Galbraith, *The Affluent Society.* Boston: Houghton Mifflin, 1976, p. 246.
7. Harry M. Caudill, *Night Comes to the Cumberlands: A Biography of a Depressed Area.* Boston: Little, Brown, 1963, pp. 333, 334.
8. Quoted in Bruce Roberts and Nancy Roberts, *Where Time Stood Still: A Portrait of Appalachia.* New York: Crowell-Collier, 1970, p. 32.

9. Quoted in Roberts and Roberts, *Where Time Stood Still,* p. 37.
10. Harrington, *The Other America,* pp. 61, 62.
11. Kenneth B. Clark, *Dark Ghetto: Dilemmas of Social Power.* New York: Harper & Row, 1965, p. 27.
12. Quoted in Kenneth B. Clark, *Dark Ghetto,* pp. 95, 96.
13. Gordon M. Fisher, "The Development and History of the U.S. Poverty Thresholds—A Brief Overview," *GSS/NSS Newsletter,* Winter 1997, pp. 6–7.

Chapter 2: Origins of the War on Poverty

14. Quoted in Dallek, *Lone Star Rising,* p. 81.
15. Lyndon B. Johnson, remarks at the University of Michigan, May 22, 1964, Lyndon Baines Johnson Library and Museum. www.lbjlib.utexas.edu/johnson/archives.hom/speeches.hom/640522.asp.
16. Quoted in Robert Dallek, *Flawed Giant: Lyndon Johnson and His Times, 1961–1973.* New York: Oxford University Press, 1998, p. 60.
17. Quoted in Dallek, *Flawed Giant,* p. 61.

18. Lyndon B. Johnson, *The Vantage Point: Perspectives of the Presidency, 1963–1969.* New York: Holt, Rinehart and Winston, 1971, pp. 73–74.

19. Johnson, *The Vantage Point,* p. 74.

20. Lyndon B. Johnson, Annual Message to the Congress on the State of the Union, January 8, 1964, Lyndon Baines Johnson Library and Museum. www.lbjlib.utexas.edu/ johnson/archives.hom/speeches. hom/640108.asp.

21. Quoted in Irving Bernstein, *Guns or Butter: The Presidency of Lyndon Johnson.* New York: Oxford University Press, 1996, p. 99.

22. Quoted in Bernstein, *Guns or Butter,* p. 99.

23. Quoted in Dallek, *Flawed Giant,* p. 76.

24. Quoted in Bernstein, *Guns or Butter,* p. 100.

25. Quoted in Dallek, *Flawed Giant,* p. 78.

26. Quoted in Bernstein, *Guns or Butter,* p. 101.

27. Johnson, *The Vantage Point,* p. 77.

28. Johnson, *The Vantage Point,* p. 81.

29. Quoted in Dallek, *Flawed Giant,* p. 78.

Chapter 3: Helping in the Community

30. James B. King, "Reinventing Government," speech to the National Association of Community Action Agencies, September 22, 1994, United States Office of Personnel Management. www.opm. gov/speeches/html/092294.htm.

31. Johnson, *The Vantage Point,* p. 74.

32. Quoted in Bernstein, *Guns or Butter,* p. 96.

33. Quoted in Irwin Unger, *The Best of Intentions: The Triumphs and Failures of the Great Society Under Kennedy, Johnson and Nixon.* New York: Doubleday, 1996, p. 82.

34. Sam Brown, "Self-Help: New Roots to an Old Idea," in Peter Shapiro, ed., *A History of National Service in America.* College Park: Center for Political Leadership and Participation, University of Maryland, 1994. James MacGregor Burns Academy of Leadership. www.academy. umd.edu/publications/National Service/vista.htm.

35. Quoted in Michael L. Gillette, *Launching the War on Poverty: An Oral History.* New York: Twayne, 1996, pp. 65–66.

36. Quoted in Robert F. Clark, *Maximum Feasible Success: A History of the Community Action Program.* Washington, DC: National Association of Community Action Agencies, 2000, p. 57.

37. Quoted in Gillette, *Launching the War on Poverty,* p. 74.

38. Quoted in Gillette, *Launching the War on Poverty,* p. 74.

39. Quoted in Robert F. Clark, *Maximum Feasible Success,* p. 60.

40. Quoted in Ralph M. Kramer, *Participation of the Poor: Comparative Community Case Studies in the War on Poverty.* Englewood Cliffs, NJ: Prentice-Hall, 1969, p. 223.

41. Quoted in Alice O'Connor, *Poverty Knowledge: Social Science, Social Policy, and the Poor in Twentieth-Century U.S. History.* Princeton, NJ: Princeton University Press, 2001, p. 169.

42. Quoted in Deb Potee and John Zelson, "Brief History of VISTA," Friends of VISTA. www.friendsofvista.org/living/hist/html.

43. Quoted in Mary E. King, "VISTA: A Vision of Social Change for the Future," in Peter Shapiro, ed., *A History of National Service in America.* College Park: Center for Political Leadership and Participation, University of Maryland, 1994. James MacGregor Burns Academy of Leadership. www.academy.umd.edu/publications/NationalService/vista.htm.

44. Sam Brown, "Self-Help."

Chapter 4: Training for Work

45. Quoted in Robert F. Clark, *The War on Poverty: History, Selected Programs, and Ongoing Impact.* Lanhan, MD: University Press of America, p.97.

46. Quoted in Christopher Weeks, *Job Corps: Dollars and Dropouts.* Boston: Little, Brown, 1967, p. 76.

47. Quoted in Robert F. Clark, *The War on Poverty,* p. 98.

48. Sar Levitan and Benjamin H. Johnston, *The Job Corps: A Social Experiment That Works.* Baltimore, MD: Johns Hopkins University Press, 1975, p. 4.

49. Quoted in Robert F. Clark, *The War on Poverty,* p. 97.

50. Quoted in Gillette, *Launching the War on Poverty,* p. 103.

51. Weeks, *Job Corps: Dollars and Dropouts,* p. 197.

52. Weeks, *Job Corps: Dollars and Dropouts,* pp. 3, 4.

53. Weeks, *Job Corps: Dollars and Dropouts,* p. 4.

54. Quoted in Gillette, *Launching the War on Poverty,* p. 180.

55. Quoted in Weeks, *Job Corps: Dollars and Dropouts,* p. 173.

56. Quoted in Sar Levitan and Garth L. Mangum, *Federal Training and Work Programs in the Sixties.* Ann Arbor, MI: Institute of Labor and Industrial Relations, 1969, pp. 194, 196.

57. Quoted in Levitan and Mangum, *Federal Training and Work Programs in the Sixties,* p. 211.

58. Quoted in Levitan and Mangum, *Federal Training and Work Programs in the Sixties,* p. 226.

59. Quoted in Levitan and Mangum, *Federal Training and Work Programs in the Sixties,* p. 217.

60. Quoted in Levitan and Mangum, *Federal Training and Work Programs in the Sixties*, p. 219.

Chapter 5: Education

61. Quoted in Edward Zigler and Susan Muenchow, *Head Start: The Inside Story of America's Most Successful Educational Experiment.* New York: BasicBooks, 1992, p. 3.
62. Quoted in Kay Mills, *Something Better for My Children: The History and People of Head Start.* New York: Dutton, 1998, p. 46.
63. Quoted in Zigler and Muenchow, *Head Start*, p. 5.
64. Quoted in Zigler and Muenchow, *Head Start*, p. 8.
65. Quoted in Zigler and Muenchow, *Head Start*, p. 6.
66. Quoted in U.S. Department of Health and Human Services: Head Start, "Creating a 21st Century Head Start: Executive Summary of the Final Report of the Advisory Committee on Head Start Quality and Expansion." www.acf.hhs.gov/programs/hsb/research/21_century/part2.htm.
67. Quoted in Mills, *Something Better for My Children*, p. 48.
68. Quoted in Zigler and Muenchow, *Head Start*, p. 24.
69. Quoted in John A. Andrew III, *Lyndon Johnson and the Great Society.* Chicago: Ivan R. Dee, 1998, p. 76.
70. Quoted in Elizabeth Brand, *Community Action at Work: TAP's Thirty-Year War on Poverty.* Blacksburg, VA: Pocahontas, 2000, p. 4.
71. Quoted in Gillette, *Launching the War on Poverty*, p. 198.
72. Quoted in Andrew, *Lyndon Johnson and the Great Society*, p. 118.
73. Quoted in Andrew, *Lyndon Johnson and the Great Society*, p. 118.
74. Lyndon B. Johnson, remarks in Johnson City, Texas, upon signing the Elementary and Secondary Education Bill, April 11, 1965, Lyndon Baines Johnson Library and Museum. www.lbjlib.utexas.edu/johnson/archives.hom/speeches.hom/650411.asp.
75. Johnson, *The Vantage Point*, p. 221.

Chapter 6: Health and Legal Services

76. Quoted in Robert F. Clark, *The War on Poverty*, p. 200.
77. Quoted in Robert F. Clark, *The War on Poverty*, p. 202.
78. Quoted in Robert F. Clark, *The War on Poverty*, p. 206.
79. Quoted in Andrew, *Lyndon Johnson and the Great Society*, p. 97.
80. Quoted in Johnson, *The Vantage Point*, pp. 212–13.
81. Quoted in Johnson, *The Vantage Point*, p. 213.
82. Quoted in Andrew, *Lyndon Johnson and the Great Society*, p. 97.
83. Quoted in Andrew, *Lyndon Johnson and the Great Society*, p. 101.
84. Johnson, *The Vantage Point*, p. 221.

85. Quoted in Gillette, *Launching the War on Poverty*, p. 253.

86. E. Clinton Bamberger, speech to National Conference of Bar Presidents, Chicago, Illinois, February 8, 1966, National Equal Justice Library. www.equaljustice library.org.cnchost.com/notable quotes.asp?category=3&action=2.

87. Quoted in Gillette, *Launching the War on Poverty*, p. 259.

Chapter 7: Civil Rights and the Great Society

88. Quoted in Richard Reeves, *President Kennedy: Profile of Power*. New York: Simon and Schuster, 1993, p. 467.

89. Quoted in Reeves, *President Kennedy: Profile of Power*, pp. 521, 522.

90. Lyndon B. Johnson, address before a joint session of Congress, November 27, 1963, Lyndon Baines Johnson Library and Museum. www.lbjlib. utexas.edu/johnson/archives.hom/ speeches.hom/631127.asp.

91. Quoted in Dallek, *Flawed Giant*, p. 61.

92. Dallek, *Flawed Giant*, pp. 113, 114.

93. Johnson, *The Vantage Point*, p. 157.

94. Johnson, *The Vantage Point*, p. 159.

95. Quoted in Maurice Isserman and Michael Kazin, *America Divided: The Civil War of the 1960s*. New York: Oxford University Press, 2000, p. 199.

96. Quoted in Isserman and Kazin, *America Divided*, p. 201.

97. Quoted in Andrew, *Lyndon Johnson and the Great Society*, pp. 59–60.

98. Quoted in Andrew, *Lyndon Johnson and the Great Society*, p. 85.

Chapter 8: Guns or Butter?

99. Quoted in Maurice Isserman, *The Vietnam War*. New York: Facts On File, 1992, p. 37.

100. Quoted in Doris Kearns, *Lyndon Johnson and the American Dream*. New York: Harper & Row, 1976, pp. 251–52.

101. Quoted in Bernstein, *Guns or Butter*, p. 526.

102. Quoted in Bernstein, *Guns or Butter*, p. 321.

103. Quoted in Bernstein, *Guns or Butter*, p. 323.

104. Quoted in Bernstein, *Guns or Butter*, pp. 528, 529.

105. Quoted in Kearns, *Lyndon Johnson and the American Dream*, p. 300.

106. Kearns, *Lyndon Johnson and the American Dream*, p. 300.

107. Quoted in Gillette, *Launching the War on Poverty*, p. 362.

108. Kearns, *Lyndon Johnson and the American Dream*, p. 337.

109. Quoted in Andrew, *Lyndon Johnson and the Great Society*, p. 195.

110. Quoted in Kearns, *Lyndon Johnson and the American Dream*, p. 344.

Chapter 9: The Legacy of the Great Society

111. Richard M. Nixon, *The Memoirs of Richard M. Nixon*. New York: Grossett & Dunlap, 1978, p. 267.

112. Nixon, *The Memoirs of Richard M. Nixon*, p. 424.
113. Quoted in U.S. Department of Transportation Federal Highway Administration, "Excerpts from the January, 1970 Issue of American Highways—The Record of the 1969 Annual Meeting." www.fhwa.dot.gov/infrastructure/build08.htm.
114. Quoted in Robert F. Clark, *The War on Poverty*, p. 65.
115. Johnson, *The Vantage Point*, p. 70.
116. Johnson, *The Vantage Point*, p. 71.
117. Johnson, *The Vantage Point*, p. 72.
118. Joseph A. Califano, "What Was Really Great About the Great Society: The Truth Behind the Conservative Myths," *Washington Monthly*, October 1999. www.washingtonmonthly.com/features/1999/9910.califano.html.
119. Johnson, *The Vantage Point*, p. 179.
120. Ronald Reagan, "Ronald Reagan Addressing a Joint Session of Congress," Ronald Reagan Information. www.presidentreagan.info/speeches/reagan_sotu_1988.cfm.
121. S.M. Miller and Martin Rein, "Will the War on Poverty Change America?" in Marc Pilisuk and Phyllis Pilisuk, eds., *How We Lost the War on Poverty*. New Brunswick, NJ: Transaction Books, 1973, pp. 187–88.
122. Quoted in Unger, *The Best of Intentions*, p. 349.
123. Quoted in Digital History, "Did the United States Lose the War on Poverty?" www.digitalhistory.uh.edu/historyonline/con_poverty.cfm.
124. Quoted in Deb Reichmann, "Wars on Poverty: Battles Exceed Wins," *Seattle Times*, July 9, 1999. www.sullivancounty.com/nf0/dispatch/war_pov.htm.
125. Robert A. Levine, "Lessons for the War on Terrorism," *International Herald Tribune*, July 26, 2002. www.rand.org/hot/op-eds/072602IHT.html.
126. Levine, "Lessons for the War on Terrorism."
127. Califano, "What Was Really Great About the Great Society."

For Further Reading

Books

Suzanne Coil, *The Poor in America*. New York: Julian Messner, 1989. A survey of poverty in the United States from the American Revolution to the late twentieth century and the challenges it presents.

Nancy Colbert, *Great Society: The Story of Lyndon Baines Johnson*. Greensboro, NC: Morgan Reynolds, 2002. An easy-to-read biography of LBJ with black-and-white photographs, a time line, and a short bibliography.

Bertha Davis, *Poverty in America and What We Do About It*. New York: Franklin Watts, 1991. This book examines who the poor are, what problems they face, and how these problems are addressed by private and government programs.

John M. Dunn, *The Civil Rights Movement*. San Diego, CA: Lucent Books, 1998. A history of the civil rights movement in the United States, from Reconstruction to the present day.

Laura K. Egendorf, *Poverty: Opposing Viewpoints*. San Diego, CA: Greenhaven Press, 1999. This book examines both sides of the various issues that make up the problem of poverty. Sources include books, newspapers, scholarly journals, government papers, and others.

Dennis Eskow, *Lyndon Baines Johnson*. New York: Franklin Watts, 1993. A well-researched basic biography of LBJ that includes photographs and an annotated bibliography.

Susan Whittlesey, *VISTA: Challenge to Poverty*. New York: Coward-McCann, 1970. The author tells the story of VISTA, how it began, what it does, and who it helps.

Websites

CongressLink, the Civil Rights Act of 1964 (www.congresslink.org/civil/essay.html). A history of the Civil Rights Act with links to relevant people, events, and terms.

Lyndon Baines Johnson Library and Museum (www.lbjlib.utexas.edu). Contains information about our thirty-sixth president and his troubled administration.

U.S. Department of Health and Human Services (www.os.dhhs.gov). Information on Head Start, Legal Services, Medicare and Medicaid, and other programs for the health, safety, and well-being of all Americans.

U.S. Department of Labor (www.dol.gov). Has information on job programs such as the Job Corps, as well as general information about employment.

Works Consulted

Books

John A. Andrew III, *Lyndon Johnson and the Great Society.* Chicago: Ivan R. Dee, 1998. This book discusses Lyndon Johnson's Great Society, its underlying philosophy, triumphs, and failures.

Irving Bernstein, *Guns or Butter: The Presidency of Lyndon Johnson.* New York: Oxford University Press, 1996. Bernstein deftly profiles Johnson as president, covering his legislative triumphs of civil rights and the Great Society, as well as the bitterness of the Vietnam War, which drained the vitality from the Texan and caused him to refuse to seek reelection.

Elizabeth Brand, *Community Action at Work: TAP's Thirty-Year War on Poverty.* Blacksburg, VA: Pocahontas Press, 2000. The story of one community's grassroots effort to fight poverty through a community action agency called TAP—Total Action Against Poverty.

Harry M. Caudill, *Night Comes to the Cumberlands: A Biography of a Depressed Area.* Boston: Little, Brown, 1963. A native of Kentucky, the author relates the history of the Cumberland Plateau from its earliest settlers to the decaying coal mining towns of the 1960s.

Rebecca Caudill, *My Appalachia.* New York: Holt, Rinehart and Winston, 1966. The author's personal reminiscences of growing up in Appalachia and her return to the region of her youth.

Kenneth B. Clark, *Dark Ghetto: Dilemmas of Social Power.* New York: Harper & Row, 1965. The author describes the social, psychological, and political structure of the urban ghetto and suggests strategies for change.

Robert F. Clark, *Maximum Feasible Success: A History of the Community Action Program.* Washington, DC: National Association of Community Action Agencies, 2000. The author tells the full story of the Community Action Program and its place in Lyndon Johnson's War on Poverty.

———, *The War on Poverty: History, Selected Programs, and Ongoing Impact.* Lanhan, MD: University Press of America, 2002. A detailed review of the history and operation of the various War on Poverty programs, including statistical charts and a bibliography.

Robert Dallek, *Flawed Giant: Lyndon Johnson and His Times, 1961–1973.* New York: Oxford University Press, 1998. Johnson's years in the White

House, the Great Society, the war in Vietnam, and his later years are explored in this second volume of Dallek's biography of LBJ.

———, *Lone Star Rising: Lyndon Johnson and His Times, 1908–1960.* New York: Oxford University Press, 1991. This first volume of Dallek's exhaustive two-volume biography details Johnson's rise from the Texas hill country to the corridors of power in Washington.

John Kenneth Galbraith, *The Affluent Society.* Boston: Houghton Mifflin, 1976. The author describes post–World War II America's "economy of abundance" and suggests that poverty remained only in isolated pockets.

Michael L. Gillette, *Launching the War on Poverty: An Oral History.* New York: Twayne, 1996. The story of how various agencies of the War on Poverty were conceived and implemented, told in the words of the individuals involved in creating those agencies.

Eric F. Goldman, *The Tragedy of Lyndon Johnson.* New York: Alfred A. Knopf, 1969. A special consultant to President Johnson, the author relates personal accounts of the daily crises, challenges, and accomplishments of the Johnson White House.

Henry Hampton and Steve Fayer, *Voices of Freedom: An Oral History of the Civil Rights Movement from the 1950s Through the 1980s.* New York: Bantam, 1991. The story of the civil rights movement as told through the words of those who participated in it.

Michael Harrington, *The Other America: Poverty in the United States.* New York: Macmillan, 1964. This book helped bring the hidden world of the poor to the attention of America and influenced Presidents Kennedy and Johnson to wage war on poverty.

Michael H. Hunt, *Lyndon Johnson's War: America's Cold War Crusade in Vietnam, 1945–1968.* New York: Hill and Wang, 1996. The author examines Lyndon Johnson's role in the Vietnam War, why he committed the United States to a far-off war, and how it ultimately ended his political career.

Maurice Isserman, *The Vietnam War.* New York: Facts On File, 1992. Discusses the roots of the Vietnam conflict, its escalation under Johnson, and its legacy. Includes numerous quotes from primary sources and a recommended reading list.

Maurice Isserman and Michael Kazin, *America Divided: The Civil War of the 1960s.* New York: Oxford University Press, 2000. The authors provide a comprehensive history of the social, political, and cultural events of the turbulent decade of the sixties.

Lyndon B. Johnson, *My Hope for America.* New York: Random House, 1964. A short book in which Johnson presents his views on many topics, including his philosophy of government.

———, *The Vantage Point: Perspectives of the Presidency, 1963–1969*. New York: Holt, Rinehart and Winston, 1971. In his own words Johnson tells of the triumphs and tragedies during his years as president. Includes black-and-white photographs, maps, letters, and documents.

Doris Kearns, *Lyndon Johnson and the American Dream*. New York: Harper & Row, 1976. Kearns, a member of LBJ's White House staff late in his presidency, writes a personal account of the powerful and energetic, but often contradictory, president.

Ralph M. Kramer, *Participation of the Poor: Comparative Community Case Studies in the War on Poverty*. Englewood Cliffs, NJ: Prentice-Hall, 1969. A detailed study of the creation, evolution, and impact of community action agencies in several California communities.

Sar Levitan and Benjamin H. Johnston, *The Job Corps: A Social Experiment That Works*. Baltimore, MD: Johns Hopkins University Press, 1975. A short history of the Job Corps written after its first decade of operation. Includes several charts and tables.

Sar Levitan and Garth L. Mangum, *Federal Training and Work Programs in the Sixties*. Ann Arbor, MI: Institute of Labor and Industrial Relations, 1969. A compilation of detailed reports evaluating various manpower programs developed in the 1960s, including the Job Corps and Neighborhood Youth Corps.

Kay Mills, *Something Better for My Children: The History and People of Head Start*. New York: Dutton, 1998. This history of Head Start includes profiles of many people involved in the program, and an in-depth look at a Head Start center in the tough Watts section of Los Angeles.

Richard M. Nixon, *The Memoirs of Richard M. Nixon*. New York: Grossett & Dunlap, 1978. Nixon's personal account of his life through his resignation of the office of president.

Alice O'Connor, *Poverty Knowledge: Social Science, Social Policy, and the Poor in Twentieth-Century U.S. History*. Princeton, NJ: Princeton University Press, 2001. The author discusses the various ways in which the "poverty problem" was thought about over the course of the twentieth century.

Marc Pilisuk and Phyllis Pilisuk, eds., *How We Lost the War on Poverty*. New Brunswick, NJ: Transaction Books, 1973. A compilation of essays on how the War on Poverty failed to achieve its objectives and how future campaigns against poverty can be more effective.

Richard Reeves, *President Kennedy: Profile of Power*. New York: Simon and Schuster, 1993. An objective, day-by-day account of John F. Kennedy's presidency, based on White House files, letters, official records, and interviews.

Bruce Roberts and Nancy Roberts, *Where Time Stood Still: A Portrait of*

Appalachia. New York: Crowell-Collier, 1970. With photographs and narrative, this book presents a look at the harsh realities of life in the poverty-stricken Appalachian region.

Irwin Unger, *The Best of Intentions: The Triumphs and Failures of the Great Society Under Kennedy, Johnson and Nixon.* New York: Doubleday, 1996. A look at the programs and people of the Great Society and how the dream ultimately came apart.

Christopher Weeks, *Job Corps: Dollars and Dropouts.* Boston: Little, Brown, 1967. The story of the beginning of the Job Corps told by the agency's deputy director.

Edward Zigler and Susan Muenchow, *Head Start: The Inside Story of America's Most Successful Educational Experiment.* New York: BasicBooks, 1992. A detailed account of the development of the Head Start program; one of the authors was a member of the original planning committee.

Periodicals

Elba K. Brown-Collier, "Johnson's Great Society: Its Legacy in the 1990s," *Review of Social Economy,* Fall 1998.

Gordon M. Fisher, "The Development and History of the U.S. Poverty Thresholds—A Brief Overview," *GSS/NSS Newsletter,* Winter 1997.

Time, "My Neighbor Needs Me," February 27, 1995.

Internet Sources

E. Clinton Bamberger, speech to National Conference of Bar Presidents, Chicago, Illinois, February 8, 1966, National Equal Justice Library. www.equaljustice library.org.cnchost.com/notable quotes.asp?category=3&action=2.

Sam Brown, "Self-Help: New Roots to an Old Idea." In Peter Shapiro, ed., *A History of National Service in America.* College Park, Maryland: Center for Political Leadership and Participation, University of Maryland, 1994. James MacGregor Burns Academy of Leadership. www.academy. umd.edu/publications/NationalServic e/vista.htm.

Joseph A. Califano, "What Was Really Great About the Great Society: The Truth Behind the Conservative Myths," *Washington Monthly,* October 1999. www.washingtonmonthly.com/ features/1999/9910.califano.html.

Digital History, "Did the United States Lose the War on Poverty?" www.digi-talhistory.uh.edu/historyonline/con_ poverty.cfm.

Lyndon B. Johnson, address before a joint session of Congress, November 27, 1963, Lyndon Baines Johnson Library and Museum. www.lbjlib. utexas.edu/johnson/archives.hom/ speeches.hom/631127.asp.

———, Annual Message to the Congress on the State of the Union, January 8, 1964, Lyndon Baines Johnson Library and Museum. www.lbjlib.utexas.edu/ johnson/archives.hom/speeches.hom/ 640108.asp.

———, "Proposal for a Nationwide War on the Sources of Poverty, Lyndon B. Johnson's Special Message to Congress, March 16, 1964," Fordham University. www.fordham.edu/halsall/mod/1964johnson-warpoverty.html.

———, remarks at the University of Michigan, May 22, 1964, Lyndon Baines Johnson Library and Museum. www.lbjlib.utexas.edu/johnson/archives.hom/speeches.hom/640522.asp.

———, remarks in Johnson City, Texas, upon signing the Elementary and Secondary Education Bill, April 11, 1965, Lyndon Baines Johnson Library and Museum. www.lbjlib.utexas.edu/johnson/archives.hom/speeches.hom/650411.asp.

James B. King, "Reinventing Government," speech to the National Association of Community Action Agencies, September 22, 1994, United States Office of Personnel Management. www.opm.gov/speeches/html/092294.htm.

Mary E. King, "VISTA: A Vision of Social Change for the Future." In Peter Shapiro, ed., *A History of National Service in America*. College Park: Center for Political Leadership and Participation, University of Maryland, 1994. James MacGregor Burns Academy of Leadership.

www.academy.umd.edu/publications/NationalService/vista.htm.

Robert A. Levine, "Lessons for the War on Terrorism," *International Herald Tribune*, July 26, 2002. www.rand.org/hot/op-eds/072602IHT.html.

Deb Potee and John Zelson, "Brief History of VISTA," Friends of VISTA. www.friendsofvista.org/living/hist/html.

Ronald Reagan, "Ronald Reagan Addressing a Joint Session of Congress," Ronald Reagan Information. www.presidentreagan.info/speeches/reagan_sotu_1988.cfm.

Deb Reichmann, "Wars on Poverty: Battles Exceed Wins," *Seattle Times*, July 9, 1999. www.sullivancounty.com/nf0/dispatch/war_pov.htm.

U.S. Department of Health and Human Services: Head Start, "Creating a 21st Century Head Start: Executive Summary of the Final Report of the Advisory Committee on Head Start Quality and Expansion." www.acf.hhs.gov/programs/hsb/research/21_century/part2.htm.

U.S. Department of Transportation Federal Highway Administration, "Excerpts from the January, 1970 Issue of American Highways—the Record of the 1969 Annual Meeting." www.fhwa.dot.gov/infrastructure/build08.htm.

Index

Picture Credits

About the Author

Craig E. Blohm has written numerous articles on historical subjects for children for the past twenty years and has authored several books for Lucent Books. He has written for social studies textbooks and conducted workshops in writing history for children. A native of Chicago, Craig and his wife Desiree live in Tinley Park, Illinois, with their two sons, Eric and Jason.